Silent No Longer

Finding My Voice After Complex Trauma

Dr. Amanda Helman

SQUARE TREE PUBLISHING
www.SquareTreePublishing.com

For more information about bulk purchases, please contact Square Tree Publishing at info@squaretreepublishing.com.

Cover design by Sharon Marta

ISBN 978-1-7369186-0-9

Learn more about Trauma in Dr. Amanda Helman's Traumaplicity Course. Want to see and hear what it looks like?

Click this video link to get a FREE video about The Power of Words from the Traumaplicity Course:
www.amandahelman.com/video

Dr. Amanda Helman provides additional information about coaching, coursework, consulting, and speaking at **www.amandahelman.com**

Endorsement

Silent No Longer is a powerful personal narrative about one woman's courage to pursue wholeness and healing after years of suffering from traumatic emotional injuries. In this book, Amanda shares her story in a thought-provoking and compelling way that will illuminate the trail of many who seek to heal from trauma. The writing in this book hosts riveting authenticity that breeds understanding for those who suffer from broken heartedness. This story will inspire you to take hold of hope and pursue healing, regardless of how deeply trauma runs in your life. There is hope!

This book is a brave and necessary re-telling of a real-life story that sings of redemption and hope through faith in God. I believe that this book will prove to be a juncture of emotional healing for many people!

Katie Luse
Executive Director, ConnectUp
www.iconnectup.net
www.katieluse.com

Katie's Grandfather was a Lt. Colonel in The Salvation Army, and the National Editor for The Salvation Army for the season, as well as the recipient of the *Order Of The Founder Award*. He did great work.

Dedication

This book is dedicated to children, teens, and adults. This book is meant to help every person who reads it identify the importance of healthy family relationships, develop ways to heal from trauma, and break current and previous generational patterns that prevent people from stepping into their true identity. You were designed to be free!

I want to thank my family, friends, relatives, and every single person that has been and will be in my life now and in the future. Every experience has led me to who I am today. You all have made an impact on my life. I am a better person because you came across my path.

Table of Contents

Chapter 1 God Knew Her Before Her Birth......................11

Chapter 2 Transitioning to High School...........................43

Chapter 3 Off Like a Wild Horse Hoping to Win.............77

Chapter 4 Relationship Decisions.......................................103

Chapter 5 The Adventure to Haiti..139

Chapter 6 Prepared to Speak the Truth.............................171

Chapter 7 New Connections...211

Chapter 8 Write Your Story, Beloved...................................257

Silent No Longer

VOICE is the roaring sound of captives being set free from bondage, complex traumas, and experiences that the body's subconscious and cellular memory may not always remember.[1] Yet God in His mercy has provided us with the ability to block most of the grievous details of what we have endured in the past. Later, however, we may have to deal with the aftermath of not being able to voice what happened in order to move forward. This book reveals my entire life's journey up to this point. These are my stories of how I gained the freedom to speak after decades of silence, and how I navigated painful experiences to find my victorious voice, leading to deep wells of liberation.

---

1. Dr. Bessel Van der Kolk, 2014

Chapter 1

I am the darkness that hides from the pain.
I want to say all is fine to hide the stain.

God Knew Her Before Her Birth

I was alive in the womb before my parents were married. Their wedding day was approximately five months before my birth. My mom said that I was often up all night ("ready to party" in her words) and slept all day. My parents had been through several traumas within their family line that they did not know would influence their new baby. Scientific research now confirms that high levels of anxiety in the mother may increase the level of cortisol washing over the baby's adrenal glands.[1] That is, if a mother has generational patterns of anxiety, those patterns transfer to the child she carries. I did not understand until much later that the negative words, anxieties, fears, tones, or experiences of my parents would also affect the level of fear or anxiety I was born with. I felt it all and heard it all.

1. Fan, Zou, Zhang, Ma, Zhang, Liu, Li et al., 2018

As a baby, I had digestive issues. I was a colicky baby, ill from drinking regular milk. After that, I was not breastfed but received soy products. I seemed no better, and perhaps, worse.[2] It is amazing that every trauma and wound can impact the emotional and physical health of the body.[3] Often, people receiving counseling to release hidden emotions trace their emotional pain to a sense of abandonment or rejection in the womb. Certainly, I was greatly affected by those beginning days of life.

Baby Years

Before God breathed that spark of life into me, He knew the purpose of my life. He knew my name would be Amanda. The name 'Amanda' in Latin means 'she who must be loved.' In Spanish, 'Amanda' means 'worthy of love.' Ironically, I did not feel worthy of love and was unable to receive love for much of my life.

My greatest weakness has now become my greatest strength. For the Almighty Lord God calls me His 'beloved.' He loves me, and I am able to receive His love. His love fills and satisfies my greatest need. Perhaps I knew this before I was born because God says, "I knew You in the womb."[4] Growing up, I had a desire for the love of Father God. My earthly father named me Amanda because of a song by the same title, recorded by the group Chicago in 1980. I know now God gave him that name for me.

2. Fan et al., 2018
3. Emotional Heath, Craig Miller, M.D.
4. Jeremiah 1:6

I narrowly escaped being born in the toilet because my father didn't believe my mother when she told him that her water had broken. My mom was getting ready to drive herself to the hospital when my dad finally realized that, yes, I was about to be born! My parents were in awe of me as a newborn. I was a healthy seven-pound baby. When I came home from the hospital, my dad held me on his chest and stared at me for hours. His time with me is my one poignant memory of how my dad really wanted to get to know me. The marvelous part of this story is that my Heavenly Papa, Lord God, gazes at me and tenderly holds me on His chest and near His heart all the time. I am in awe of this! I want to look at my Heavenly Papa and gaze back at His loving eyes because they are so bright, pure, and genuine.

I don't remember much of my first few months on earth, but I heard stories about how my uncle, my mom's brother, would spend lots of nights and days watching me and taking care of me. This sense of his care melts my heart. I realize my uncle was like a healthy father figure to me as an infant.

My first two years of life are a blur. I lived with my parents in Allentown, PA and I vaguely remember being at the apartment with the small backyard. When I was two and a half years old, my sister Melissa was born. I have a picture of myself holding my sister while my mom was in the hospital. I remember the joy I felt because she was born.

Finding Home

When I turned three, my parents parked our car in front of a big house, which became our new home. The two-story dwelling, initially used as a veterinary hospital for horses, had a large yard. I had no idea at the time that this house (an affordable blessing for my parents) would be such a place of unrest. My big bedroom was across the hall from my sister's room. I do not remember much about being a three-year-old, but I have some memories as a four-year-old when I had play dates with one of the neighborhood boys in my bedroom.

As a little girl, I often sang, "Jesus loves me." I grew up Lutheran, baptized with a sprinkling of water. In Sunday school, I sang about Jesus and learned stories about Him. In my bedroom at home, I would often sing to Jesus as a way to remember all of the fun that I had in the classes at church. I am not sure exactly when my memories at the house became grey or hard to remember, but by age four, much of my childlike nature had quickly dwindled, and I was not sure why at the time.

Squeaky

One day while I was in preschool, a brown and white beagle dog showed up on our porch. My mom let me give him a toy pretzel, and because it squeaked, I named him Squeaky. My parents decided to keep Squeaky, and he became my beloved dog; however, I also deeply feared Squeaky because when I ran past him, he would always try to bite my ankles. Squeaky barked a lot, but he became a valued member of the family.

During early childhood, my dad's great Uncle Manwell and his wife would often visit. I remember going to their house sometimes, and they would visit our house. I slept over at their house once, and I have a dim memory of someone coming towards me in a dark room at night. He called me 'Mandy.' For years, I shuddered inside when I heard this name spoken. Sometime between ages three and five, I began wetting my pants. I was not sure whether it was an issue at preschool or during kindergarten. I went on a trip to West Virginia with Uncle Jack and his wife, and the only thing I can remember was that I wet my pants on the trip.

Following the trip to West Virginia, I was a flower girl at my mom's cousin's wedding. I was nervous as I walked down the aisle, keeping in step with the music. I was quirky then, and I cannot remember feeling much joy, just anxiety and fear. God has since reminded me that I was His princess back then, and He found ways to honor me in the most troubling situations in childhood and adolescence. For example, I was a flower girl at several weddings, so I pretended that I was a princess.

I was fortunate to have Sarah, a good friend at preschool. She lived in the house behind our garage. I was really looking forward to starting kindergarten with Sarah, but I was devastated when I found out that she would be moving away before school started. Sarah and I exchanged letters for some time, but I never saw her again. This loss marked a difficult season for me, because the rest of my story contains so much rejection. Sarah was a friend I would have chosen to remain in my life.

Kindergarten

I still have the picture of myself smiling on the first day of kindergarten. My birthday falls on August 29th, so I began school as an almost five-year-old. I, of course, loved it. I loved going shopping for school clothes in the summer. My mom would buy me pretty dresses and fancy glimmering shoes. I loved getting all dolled up at this age.

My kindergarten teacher, ironically, had also taught my mom. We came from a small town. If your family lived there long enough, you might get the same teacher that your parents had. In class, I loved watching *The Letter People*, a reading series on television featuring different letter names and sounds. I remember the odd snacks they'd sometimes give us. One day, we had prunes with orange juice. We had other snacks, but I remember this as the worst! Even though I only went to school half-day, I often peed my pants, although I could not figure out why (until much later). My kindergarten years were an overall positive experience despite the incontinence issues.

About this time, my parents were expecting another baby. I'd often hear my parents fight, but I cannot remember what about. My dad worked at a hospital, and my mom stayed home taking care of Squeaky and us girls. I remember the holidays being a favorite time for me, visiting with my grandparents and great-grandparents. My great-grandparents (my Nana's parents) lived up the street from our house. My great-grandparents would come to my Nana's home for Thanksgiving and Christmas. My great grandmother gave us sweet little gifts, such as dolls, on Christmas Eve. Following trips to Nana's, we would visit Great Uncle Bill and his brother Ben during the holidays. These two bravely fought during World War II. My Uncle Bill received a Purple Heart. He was shot in the chest, fortunately falling backward into a cold lake, which saved his life. I spent time at my great grandparents' house in Allentown, close to the hospital where I was born. I would sit on the couch, staring in fascination at the picture of a Catholic crucifix hanging on the wall. Every time I visited my great grandparents, my eyes would gravitate to that picture. Many times, we sat, eating cashews, looking at all of the photos of our family in picture books or hanging on the walls of the living room. Oh, how I loved to study all of the pictures on that wall! Our final destination would be at my Pappy's (mom's dad) parents. They had a cute home next to a big yard, and the family would have picnics there.

Nana and Pappy

After my sister was born, I would sometimes stay overnight at Nana's. My grandparents lived in a delightful three-story house. Pappy would sit in his recliner and watch TV. When it was too warm outside, my grandparents would close the doors to the TV room to keep the cold air inside. If you left, Pappy made sure you shut the door. He was the King of the Recliner. Sometimes I would sit in his recliner and giggle, and he would say, "Hey there, that's my chair," usually jokingly (yet not kidding). My Nana would sit in the other recliner, and my aunt would be on the extra sofa. I remember we would stay up to watch Nick at Night. Some of my favorite shows were Patty Duke, My Three Sons, and Dobie Gillis. I slept beside my Nana and Pappy's bed on a sofa-bed. The sheets always smelled clean like Nana's laundry detergent. Usually, she would put Coca-Cola sheets on the sofa-bed just for me. In the morning, she made little pancakes and eggs for breakfast. My favorite part was adding butter and syrup to the pancakes and then letting the ketchup from my eggs all mix together. Somehow, that doesn't sound very appetizing now, but it warms my heart to remember those days fondly. I sometimes have the urge to go to my Nana's so that she can make those little pancakes again.

I adore my Pappy. I remember his laughter as I sat outside on the porch with him and Nana. He had been a cook in the Navy, and he still is an amazing baker. He cooked for all the holidays, picnics, and birthdays. My favorite part of Pappy's baking was that he would make me a special Strawberry Shortcake for my birthday.

At that time, I loved everything about Strawberry Shortcake, My Little Pony, Barbie, and She-Ra. As a little girl,

Pappy was someone I looked up to and cherished. He would always have his video camera handy to capture family memories during the holidays. We loved to watch the holiday VHS tapes when we were all together.

The Gradual Loss of Voice

I cannot tell you the exact moment that the slow progression toward the death of my innocent childhood began, but somewhere in those years between three and five years of age, I gradually 'lost my voice,' and good sense of identity. I stopped communicating my true feelings, wants, and needs. I quickly transitioned into the role of an adult. Often my mom would ask me for advice about what to do in life situations. I became more like an adult at an age when I should have been a carefree child. The fighting between my parents continued, and my mother frequently cried after all the shouting had ended. I was too young to truly grasp it all, but I knew my mom seemed trapped in an abusive marriage that was taking its toll on her. She did not know how to get help or leave the situation, and I am sure she was in a state of terror.

I did not recognize at the time how painful and disheartening all this fighting was to me. The birth of my baby brother did not change things. I remember during one fight, my mom carried a steaming Salisbury steak dish in one hand and held my baby brother in the other arm, with my sister standing next to her. Sobbing, my mother looked me in the eyes and asked me if she should take all of us and leave my father. She looked desperate for an answer. I said what any five-year-old child would say to their mother: "No." In my heart, our family staying together was essential to me. At that moment, I quickly learned to be an adult. After that, I would often try to speak up during fights, yet I was fearful because my dad made awful verbal threats. He would frequently lunge at me to get me to shut up. I would close my eyes or flinch. If I did say something, he ran toward me to hit me. So I just stopped speaking up. My mom often cried at night; she was very lonely because my dad would be out drinking or partying late into the night.

Rejection from Peers

In first grade, I experienced rejection from my peers. I am sure the effects of the trauma I was experiencing at home changed my personality and how I responded. I was picked on routinely and connected less and less with my classmates. I felt alone. My only friend, Sarah, was no longer there to share my feelings with, so in hopes of forming new friend-ships, I tried to please other kids by giving away items from my lunch box or making an effort to join in something fun at lunchtime.

The rejection and mistreatment by others made me feel like an outcast early in life. I was always picked last during gym class and I would often be silent in small groups because I felt ignored, that no one would listen to my idea. I couldn't seem to fit in no matter what I did. I became numb, and the pain kept getting pushed deeper within me. I fantasized about becoming a famous, beautiful actress someday. This fantasy was one of many I created to escape the painful reality of my home life. I was quite a dreamer. I wanted to sing, dance, and be recognized for my talent.

Dark Hours

I am not sure when it began, but I began to develop crushes on boys at an unusually early age. I dreamt of marrying some of them. At the time, I'm not sure why, but I even had dreams in which I would have full-blown sex with one of the boys I had a crush on in class. This kind of dreaming was not usual at such a young age, but I never told anyone. I often had sexual dreams about boys. I never discussed these dreams at home, nor was anything like this brought up, but I remember masturbating, recognizing that touching myself or humping the couch felt good at this young age.

To add to the fear and tumult, I developed a fear of witches at this same time. Every time I heard the sound of the train on the railroad tracks nearby, I would panic, thinking that witches were coming to harm me. This worrisome problem led to a deep fear of the dark. I was often afraid and would wrap myself up tightly under the covers at night. But I also still loved being in church during this time. I prayed to Jesus frequently. One time after I accidentally said the name of Satan instead of Jesus, I believed the lie that Jesus would not forgive me and that I now belonged to the enemy.

The torment in my mind, heart, and soul vividly increased during this year. The spirit of fear intensified, along with sadness, grief, condemnation, and self-hatred. I was living in a traumatic environment where no place was safe, including school. I tried to imagine being safe, but I still struggled with feeling afraid. I even felt isolated from God and rejected by Him.

Self-Protection

Losing your voice—or the ability to speak up for yourself—without realizing it is devastating, especially for a little girl. I did not know that I still had a voice, but it was silenced and hidden. At the time, I had no idea that Amanda Lynn, who was born to live in this world, was currently dead inside me. I was literally a shell and simply went through the motions of life, not sure anyone had even taken notice. I certainly was not part of the popular crowd. *Trauma has a way of turning people into the walking dead*. Classmates at school silenced me with hurtful comments. Peers avoided selecting me to be on their team during gym class. However, I loved my gym teacher so much, Mr. Pixie, or Mr. PeeFly, as we endearingly called him. This little six-year-old was crying on the inside for help, love, acceptance, and a sense of belonging.

Things seemed blurred in so many ways…memories, thoughts. All I knew was to hide inside myself. My inner conscience locked all the painful, hidden trauma away until much later when it came to light through my journey of discovery. Overeating became a way of safely numbing my pain. I had been noticeably gaining weight during second grade. My relatives from both sides of the family overate during all holidays, a bad habit I'd learned as well. I was trying to hide something, but I did not know it was my voice. I felt as if my vocal cords were damaged, and I could not speak. To stay safe, I spent much time hiding in my thoughts and not knowing how to share my thoughts with anyone around me.

I realize now, using food for comfort and weight gain were unconscious attempts to insulate; to try to protect myself.[5] My heart did not want to admit something horrible had happened to me when I was a little child. Children rarely realize the truth of sexual abuse and complex trauma; they live their lives in denial, avoiding the fact. However, sexual abuse severely damages the core identity of anyone who falls victim to it.

Hiding in Food

I noticeably continued to gain weight. In fact, there came a point when my entire family spoke to me about my weight gain. I was a young girl with deep emotional pain and wounds, but nobody was able to identify the trauma beneath the extra weight I was carrying, nor hear my silent inner screams. I was trying to hide something, and I did not know it was my responsibility to speak up about the unspeakable. Perhaps I was hiding so I wouldn't have to face the abuse

---

5. Bannon, Selwen, & Hymowitz, 2018

I had suffered at a young age. Young children often do not have the words to speak about their traumatic experiences. I couldn't remember the details of the abuse I suffered back then, and it would take years for me to consciously deal with it, but I was trying to numb the pain of the harm done to me.

The heart of a little child does not want to admit what really happened. Young children are so resilient, often disso-ciating events as a type of 'Band-Aid' for such wounds.[6] The reality of these situations maybe so overwhelming, many children even die.[7] Girls are more likely than boys to ad-mit the truth about sexual abuse later in life, but still many avoid the truth for decades because it is buried deep within the subconscious mind.[8] Facing the painful reality of sexual abuse and processing the aftermath is a lot of work. Trauma severely damages the core identity of the human psyche.

Transition to Girl Scouts

The annual Girl Scout bridging ceremony took place just before first grade. I had enjoyed being in the troop of Brownies that met in my church. But, the coming transition meant that I would attend Girl Scouts at the Catholic church near my home. I was nervous and quite a bit scared at that first meeting. As I listened to the new leaders, I suddenly began to cry. I don't even know what I was crying about, but another little girl was crying, too. The leaders started

6. Barnes, 2018
7. Felitti, Andra, Nordenburg, Williamson, Spitz, Edwards, Koss & Marks, 1998
8. Priebe & Svedin, 2008; Van de Kolk, 2018

comforting the other little girl but did not come over to me. Feelings of rejection, abandonment, and unworthiness arose within me. I couldn't understand why I got ignored on the first day. After the meeting, I was still crying and told my mom that I did not want to go back. Thankfully, my mom respected my decision to stop attending Girl Scouts. I often wondered what triggered my response, but it was a painful fore-shadowing of what was to come throughout the remaining school years. Rejection was very familiar to me. At an early age, my false core beliefs whispered that I was not worthy of love, attention, protection, or important enough to be heard. I accepted these beliefs and allowed other people to treat me this way because that was all I knew.

In second grade, I realized I was acting out my response to complex trauma. I heard my second-grade teacher talk about what is a 'good touch' and what is 'not a good touch' and I felt a conviction. Well, I had conviction, but it immediately led to condemnation. I did not know it was wrong until my second-grade teacher told our class about the difference between good touching and bad touching. As soon as I heard those words, I was enveloped in dismay and condemnation. The dreadful feelings of guilt, anger, shame, and grief at this realization were so overwhelming that I began having nightmares about it. I told no one about my frightening conviction, and as a result, this secret tormented me for almost two decades. Since my focus was solely on this act, self-condemnation overrode the trauma I had experienced as a little girl. I often wept because I believed I was a terrible person. I still had crushes on boys and focused my ongoing attention towards boys, but no one was willing to notice me or recognize me as a valid person of worth. I frequently heard about how bad I was in school and at home.

Early on, I was not a popular girl at school, and I suffered rejection as other students began bullying me. This unkind treatment was a grievous insult to my already-wounded heart. I never fought back or stood up for myself. I just took the mistreatment, silently hiding my pain inside. That summer, I invited several girls from school to my birthday party. No one showed up. My mom began calling some of the girls' parents, but no one came to my home that day. Sharp pangs of rejection and sorrow hit me deeply. I sobbed from grief, and the embarrassment was like another painful dagger thrown at my heart. I wore the aftereffects of rejection, condemnation, shame, and neglect like badges. My thoughts repeated a litany of unworthiness. The stronghold named 'unworthy' clinched the core of my soul as I agreed with the voices in my head.

I lived in a dysfunctional environment with daily exposure to my dad's heavy drinking, staying out late in the evenings, and fighting with my mom when he returned home. Everywhere I went, people told me I was unlovable and that I was not worth being cared for by anyone. My mom was trying her best to love me, but I now know she felt trapped in her own painfully abusive situation.

I had front row seats to my parents' almost constant disputes, and it was gradually shaping my perception of how men should treat women. My heart became shredded into minuscule pieces. I kept sinking lower into a place of darkness. I would often cry out to Jesus at night, but I felt so far from Him as I sang the hymns from church. I felt disconnected from Him, from myself, and others. This scenario was replayed daily and increased in intensity at a rapid pace.

During second grade, my parents had a falling out with my great Uncle Manwell. They did not speak to him again and only saw him during our large, infrequent family reunions. The last time he came to the house when I was young, he brought me a three-foot toy bear. I kept it in my room for years. None of my family members thought this unusual at the time nor could they recognize the signals of sexual abuse. When I was a child, I had twenty to twenty-five toy animals on my bed, which provided a semblance of comfort for me most of my childhood and throughout my teenage years. I did not connect the events with my distant relative Uncle Manwell until later in my story

In my early teens, God slowly began to reveal the truth about my sexual abuse. I was sitting on my front porch one day, mulling over my feelings of condemnation when I heard a small audible voice mention my Uncle Manwell. The thought was, "Uncle Manwell sexually abused you," in the faintest voice possible enough for me to keep tucked away for decades. God knew that I did not have the cognitive ability to remember or process what happened with Uncle Manwell.

Hope in Creative Writing

During fourth grade, my creative side began to emerge as my fourth-grade teacher, Mr. Alley, told us about his journeys to Japan. He was an exceptional teacher. Mid-year, I had this brilliant idea to write and direct class plays. As soon as the first script was ready, I shared the plays with other students in the class. Initially, this sparked conversations with other kids who would not normally give me the time of day. There was also another unpopular classmate whose interest was piqued by this new venture. However, soon after I revealed the scripts, other students attempted to direct the play, compete for the leading roles, and essentially twist my original ideas. Because my voice was lost deep inside me, I became silent. I allowed these peers to hijack my plays because I craved acceptance and love. After a week of writing scripts, Mr. Alley halted the scriptwriting because everyone was fighting over who was going to do what in the play, which interrupted class time.

The remainder of the year was a blur except for Japanese Culture day. I still remember the taste of my first piece of Japanese candy. It was wrapped in rice paper that deliciously melted in my mouth. To this day, I remember loving every minute of this new cultural experience and can remember the stations, the Japanese dresses, and the Japanese maps. My love for culture had begun!

Saying The Good News

One of my friends, Jen, was my neighbor, and we used to hang out at each other's houses. We munched on salt and vinegar chips and became 'blood sisters' by using red nail polish instead of real blood for a friendship pact. What a delightful time! I had been attending church and enjoyed singing hymns and listening to the music. Gradually, I began telling her about my love for Jesus Christ. One Sunday, Jen came to church with me and eventually brought her family, too. I was so pleased that she was learning more about Jesus. Our talk together was my first occasion to serve as an evangelist. I was able to talk about Jesus Christ without any altar calls or an explanation of the gospel by the pastor.

Many families, even those that grew up in the church, did not always hear the 'good news' except perhaps on holidays. I am sure I gave the most basic explanation of the gospel, but God knew what He was doing with me back then. Jen and I frequently spoke about Jesus. One day, we had a conversation about how once someone gets free, they need to keep the house (body) free from returning demons.[9] What I did not tell her was that I was terrified after reading that Scripture because I had been hearing voices and was so afraid of darkness and demons. I did not know this at the

---

9. John 5:14

time, but these events were trying to unravel one of my callings later in life: to set the captives free.

Swimming was one of my favorite activities. During summer breaks, I spent most of my time at the pool with my mom and siblings. Due to my fears, I was often afraid that the Jaws shark might be in the pool. Thanks to the movie Jaws and my vivid imagination, I believed it was possible. Some of the other kids had the same idea, but I was a little extreme in thinking that a shark could survive in clear, salt-free water.

Often, we would return to the pool in the evenings for free swim. The snack bar had my favorite snacks, Swedish Fish and Hot Dollars. I continued to use food to hide my pain. My parents did not recognize this as a coping mechanism because they were also using food to try to fill their emotional needs. ***The root of self-destructive behaviors is sometimes difficult to identify. Prayer, guidance, and self-searching are essential to the process of self-discovery,*** something that I did not realize until much later.

Transition to Middle School

I began my middle school journey in fifth grade. I had an exceptional reading ability and always worked hard. I took the time to process information, and as a perfectionist, I spent hours studying so that I could get excellent grades and gain acceptance. I continued to be unusually quiet during classes, never rediscovering my voice at all during my time at school. That year, I had many crushes on boys. One of them actually spit on me during class! I did not say anything about it as I took on the shame—it was part of my identity; I thought I deserved mistreatment and embarrassment. I believed I was not valuable. Although I was eager to build friendships, I was still not popular in middle school.

I really enjoyed reading, but it was also a coping mechanism. During the holidays, I would curl up on the couch, reading all the books given to me in just one or two days. There was no safe place at school or at home. I did not have any friends and did not feel safe to share how I was feeling at school. There was no one I felt safe enough to connect with across any of these environments. My dad would often call me names as I was an unwilling witness of my parents' ongoing arguments at home. The cycle continued through all my school days.

My love for reading was part of what saved my sanity during middle school. I read books as a stress-reliever. I also found some relief by playing the clarinet in the school band. Singing, dancing, theatre, and creative arts were a necessary part of my life, but I would often get shy and clam up. I was too nervous when I tried out for the leading roles in theatre, but I enjoyed being part of the chorus. I did have one opportunity to play the female lead during middle school, and it made my year special.

The summer before sixth grade was excruciating. My parents fought so much. I watched lots of soap operas with Nana or my family, and through those shows, I lived a fantasy life. I was often angry and bossy with my brother and sister. This situation stems back to when I was younger and had to make adult decisions and fill the role of caretaker for my siblings. They told me later that I was like a mom and stepped into a position that I did not need to fulfill. I had a tremendous amount of self-hatred, and I was not very kind to my siblings due to all the anger, frustration, and envy. My popular sister was a cheerleader and had many friends visiting our house. By contrast, I seemed like a non-entity.

During my school years, I was literally eating my life away, and no one knew what to do with me, besides belittling me with unkind words. Since I was afraid of the dark, I would turn on a nightlight and hide in bed with the covers up to my neck. So many times, I thought I heard the sound of footsteps going down the hallway. I was always afraid of the train noises at night and thought there were witches out to get me. I also saw disturbing faces in the wood paneling in my room. I didn't like looking at the faces, but I still did anyway, even though it gave me the creeps. I would often pray or cry. Just before sixth grade, I was at the pinnacle of what could have been my demise: I was at my heaviest weight. Due to the silent dysfunction of my family, I often went to school with knots in my hair, looking like a disheveled mess. I did not realize how much depression I was suffering then, but in retrospect, the situation was not a good one. My family never said anything to me about depression.

Horrible Conversations

One summer, my parents were fighting more than usual. My dad had just returned from a business trip that night. He told me that none of us should come upstairs because he and my mom were going to have sex. I do not recall him ever saying anything like this to me before this situation. I was terrified by that thought, and I could not sleep all night. I stayed downstairs in the living room. For some reason, deep inside myself, I feared for my safety.

People made fun of me even more at school, and the depression and sadness grew. Although living, I was an empty shell. One day, the knots in my hair were so apparent that some girls came over to make fun of me. Clearly, no one in a position of authority knew how to address the underlying issues. The middle school students were so mean, and now I understand that it was all they knew at the time.

I had one teacher whom I want to thank today, Mrs. Varconi. She was troubled about me and called for a meeting with my parents to tell them about her concerns. My parents, due to their own trauma and lack of self-awareness, did not agree and assured her I was okay. In reality, I was not. My parents told me about their conversation, which just echoed all of the voices I had heard at night; angry voices repeating my fears, rejection, loneliness, and confirming my persona as an outcast.

A New Pen Pal

Soon after this awkward conversation, Mrs. Marconi told our class that we were to have pen pals. I was ecstatic! I could not wait to find out who my pen pal would be that year. When I opened my first letter, I was pleased to see a photo of a beautiful Latina girl from Allentown. Her letter seemed friendly, and she also sent a picture of her brother. I was thrilled and could not wait to write back to her! I was looking forward to having a new friend with whom I could share my life that year. I showed my mom the letter. Unfortunately, she was afraid that the girl and her brother were going to harm me because they were Latino. She told me that I could not have her as a pen pal. My heart broke. My mom's racism had stemmed from my Nana and Pappy. I did not enjoy going shopping with Nana because she would make fun of Black people and Latinos. I just wanted to hide. I thought that wasn't right, and I often told her so. I was very upset because I wanted to remain pen pals with the Latina girl, but I could not tell Mrs. Marconi the truth because I was embarrassed. I just told her that I didn't want a pen pal. Her face showed surprise at my request, but she did respect my wishes.

I wrote some stories that year. Mrs. Marconi once had me read a story to the class. The story was about peanut butter (still my favorite food), and I am sure it did not make much sense. I wish I still had that nonsensical story to re-read today. Nevertheless, Mrs. Marconi did what she could to help me find my voice. I am thankful that she did notice me and that she cared. Sixth grade is generally a rough year for most adolescents. My battle with depression, anxiety, and loneliness that year was one of the most difficult that I have experienced to date.

The Saving Grace of Field Hockey

However, the best decision I made that year was to sign up for field hockey, which was a lifesaver for me. I got my equipment early and practiced running during the summer. When I was not spending many depressing hours up in the attic, just staring into space, I went outside to run.

Again, due to our dysfunctional family at the time, my first day of field hockey with the team was another day of great embarrassment for me. I arrived on the first day wearing the wrong clothes, a tee-shirt, and jeans with sneakers. I was sure the junior high and high school girls were making fun of me throughout practice and sprinting and doing all kinds of exercises in my jeans was very difficult. To top it off, my middle school gym teacher, Mrs. Miller, was on the field as the high school field hockey coach. She told me to tie my shoes in front of everyone during gym class. I just froze. Because I hesitated, she made me sit on the ground while she tied them. That day was an awful day of humiliation. During practice, I felt a sense of freedom engaging in drills and exercise. After the day was over, I made sure to get some better workout clothing. I had been mostly sedentary up until this point in my life, and I had a rough time getting in shape. However, this sport became a huge part of my life that helped me survive and gave me back a small spark of joy and hope. I was passionate about this sport and played on the defense. During one of the games, I won a field hockey stick for being an excellent defender. Until that point, I had not won anything in my life besides a race I ran in first grade. I was on cloud nine for several weeks! I had received affirmation for my abilities! I began working out and improving my skills. My area of concern was to strive and do well so that others would want to see me, know me, and be a part of my life. I tried so hard for these little triumphs. I spoke with some of the girls during field hockey but didn't establish any solid friendships. I just could not put my finger on why I felt so disconnected from life.

Ongoing Negative Words

During sixth grade, my home life had not drastically changed. My parents were still fighting, my cheerleader sister was still popular, and my brother was starting school. I was still verbally abusive to my brother and sister at home because I was full of bitterness, resentment, anger, self-hatred, and rejection. I had come to believe I was unworthy of any love. This poison was spewing out of me at home, where I could show anger, but I did not realize how much anger I was internalizing. My dad would often scream at us if he could not find his shoes. He would chase us around the table if we talked back to him, or he would act like he was going to hit us. I heard him call us stupid, "f***ing idiots," "basket cases," dumb, fat, and sometimes the word c***. The words hit my heart like a punch every time I heard them until I finally went numb. I must have been in shock as these word curses kept hitting me. I took the brunt of shame and ridicule at home and school. There was no one place I could go where I felt safe. I learned how to protect myself by covering my heart and over-feeding my body with food. I still fought against the voices I was hearing, but I felt a murderous spirit tormenting me at night. I felt very scared, but too frightened to tell anyone. I did not have many friends besides my friend, Jen.

At the end of sixth grade, my mom began a new job working night shifts. I didn't know it, but my dad was on heavy doses of cocaine and alcohol then. At one point, he punched my mom in the face, and she had a black eye the next day. My grandfather was so upset with him. My mom had to wear makeup to cover over the bruises on her eye. That was the first time I saw my mom with a black eye, and it added more shock and fear to my already dead and numb heart. My dad had been working his own business, but after this year, he ended up overdosing on cocaine and alcohol. He spent three months on the couch, and my grandparents came to help us while my mom worked the night shift. I didn't understand what was happening, but I knew my family was not okay. No matter how we all tried to cope, it was not working.

Then the situation got worse. Several months later, my dad got a new job. However, right around this time, my mom started acting weird and annoying. One time, we were supposedly on the way to get toothpaste at the store, but my mom circled the block ten times because she didn't want to get out of the car. I was so upset because I didn't understand what she was afraid of at that point. She began to stay in the house all the time. She cried a lot, and she would repeatedly wash her hands, which was one more thing that was hard for me to process. I was so frustrated because she wouldn't stop.

My dad continued to be verbally abusive to us all, and we had to endure these circumstances day in and day out. During one fighting match, my dad told my mom she was worthless and that she had to get better. My brother, sister, and I watched in shock as he spat on our mother in front of us. My mom began sobbing because she was very germ conscious. That spiteful scene was horrible to watch. I was learning from my only male role model what kind of treatment to expect from a man. Even though I painfully agreed again with this false belief, deep down, I hoped it was not true, but it was all I could see at that point. My little heart was devastated. A few years later, my mom told us that my uncle had advised her to get help because if she didn't, he and my aunt would take us away. That moment was my mom's turning point because she did not want to lose her children. She did get help, and during the next year, she regained some of her health, but I am not sure my mom has ever been the same since that year. She still washes her hands obsessively. I think she witnessed something that sent her into a state of shock that resulted in feelings of powerlessness. The handwashing was the way she began to cope. I have more empathy and compassion for her today, but I was so angry growing up. I was very angry with her for staying in that dysfunctional dilemma and subjecting us all to this mess. I just did not understand it at all.

While all of this was going on, during seventh and eighth grade, I was just as unpopular. I was mistreated at school, made fun of, ignored, and generally abused wherever I went. I was so hungry for real love I ran towards anyone who gave me the faintest affirmation.

I was still playing field hockey in seventh and eighth grade and loved this part of my life. Even though the sprints, the practice, and the games were enjoyable, I was full of insecurities and doubts about my abilities. I continued to experience rejection and abuse from people, even coaches. Living with shame, fear, humiliation, and doubt was a way of life for me. I did not know what else to do at the time, and I did not admit the deep pain I was feeling.

In eighth grade, I joined the marching band and made some friends. At practice, I sat near a saxophone player who was funny and goofy, and my friend Ali, who played the flute, became a lifelong friend. We talked on the bus and enjoyed participating in the halftime show on the football field. I was enjoying all of the quirky, creative people I met. Despite that, I still did not quite fit in the band.

Painful Life Struggles

I started catechism classes during eighth grade, which would lead up to taking my first communion, according to Lutheran tradition. My class spent Sundays with Pastor Gifford, a spiritual father in my life. During class, I often drew pictures of wedding dresses because I always imagined scenarios of my future wedding. I often dreamed about being a bride, enjoying a wonderful marriage, and having children. These vignettes were part of my fantasy and daydream life, which was my escape on good days and bad. This year, more torment began in my mind, as I was still carrying so much guilt about my trauma responses and the awful events that happened as a child.

The Attack On My True Identity

I began having thoughts about women. I would watch TV and think that women were more attractive than men. That thought was horrifying, so I looked for magazine pictures of men and would stare at them for a long time, trying to muster some sense of attraction for them. I was always thinking about this and felt the extreme torment of terror and fear. I did not realize at the time, but this is an enemy tactic. He will condemn or try to aggravate fear and obsession about any thought he can use to snare someone and establish a pitfall to pull the focus away from Papa God. That fear is like an arrow shot powerfully into the brokenness and soul wounds. His best shots are toward children during the vulnerability of the early years. This misery was my experience, I came to reject my own feminine design. Rejection

40

caused a deep, festering wound in my soul. I agreed with the enemy's lies about my identity—spiritually, sexually, emotionally, and physically. God kept calling me toward Him, but I was in a numb state. I was seeking God's heart and presence but had no clue how to run to Him. Some words from my favorite hymn I sang in desperation to know Him were:

"Lamb of God, You take away the sin of the world,
have mercy on us; Lamb of God,
you take away the sins of the world,
Grant us peace, grant us peace."

Masten A, Barnes A. Resilience in Children: Developmental Perspectives. Children. July 2018:98. doi:10.3390/children5070098

Felitti, V. J., Anda, R. F., Nordenberg, D., Williamson, D. F., Spitz, A. M., Edwards, V., Koss, M. P., & Marks, J. S. (1998). Relationship of childhood abuse and household dysfunction to many of the leading causes of death in adults: The Adverse Childhood Experiences (ACE) Study. American Journal of Preventive Medicine, 14(4), 245–258. https://doi.org/10.1016/S0749-3797(98)00017-8

Priebe, G. & Swedin, C. G. (2008). Childhood sexual abuse is largely hidden from adult society. An epidemiological study of adolescents' disclosures. Child Abuse & Neglect, 32, 1095-1108.

Silent No Longer

.

Chapter 2

I want to get out of this pit.
Why is it so dark, and I can't sit?

Transitioning to High School

I had hoped for new beginnings in high school. However, in those first weeks of the new school year, I realized that everything was still the same, and the situation was not likely to change anytime soon. I continued to feel trapped in that suffocating box labeled the 'quiet nice girl' who seemed to be unaffected by insults and ridicule. That was simply not true, but even so, I allowed people to humiliate me. Teachers often have no clue about the subtle bullying that occurs in school. For instance, during class one day, a guy thoroughly demoralized me with belittling statements such as, "you are ugly and fat," but I didn't speak up to defend myself. His responses were so subtle that it was not noticed by my teacher. My voice was stuck. I had unwittingly enabled people to treat me with disrespect, dishonor, and contempt. There seemed to be a sign tattooed across my forehead, saying, "Please harm and insult me." I felt helpless, not knowing how to reverse the situation. I lived for decades in an atmosphere of condemnation, believing that all my improper behavior deserved punishment. I was so confused because I still had disturbing sexual dreams about females. I told no one, but I was horrified by these recurring unwanted thoughts. I would sob and pray to God for the ability to look at men and be sexually attracted to them. Yet, I also had many emotional-based crushes on guys and spent a lot of time imagining scenarios about them in my fantasy world of escape. It was such a confusing time.

The trauma of torment and rejection occurred across all areas of my life. Fortunately, my enjoyment of field hockey, marching band, and chorus helped me escape the dysfunction at home. I also signed up for theatre, which was something I always dreamed of doing, although shyness prevented me from getting the full benefit of the experience.

Thankfully, I was glad to be busy in the evenings with band and field hockey, yet my doubts and insecurities about my athletic abilities often ruled my thoughts. During summer practice, I hung out with some of the girls from the team. We would either go to my grandparents for lunch or over to another friend's house. My grandparents lived across the street from the practice field, so I enjoyed running over to visit them between practices. My grandmother would make me a grilled cheese sandwich. I enjoyed the combination of melty grilled cheese in the air-conditioned living room while I watched The Young and the Restless with my grandmother. What a blast! Today, I can't believe I watched soap operas.

Food Frustrations

My frustration increased when I realized I was still using food for comfort. I would overeat and then despise myself afterward. I started fasting or drinking protein meal shakes on certain days. Most of my life, I had a body image distortion, where I could not view my body accurately. I avoided the cafeteria most of the time, opting to have lunch in the home economics room with one of my favorite, safe teachers, Mrs. Heavenly. Other students ate lunch in her room, too, in this friendly environment. Whenever I did head to the cafeteria, I had an awkward time figuring out where to sit and with whom. On good days, I was able to sit in the lunchroom with my band friends. We made up code names for our crushes. On one not-so-good day, when I went to the cafeteria, there was a baby-picture contest, and someone commented that my baby picture looked like an alien. That statement was only one of an onslaught of comments that wounded my heart deeply. There seemed to be an agenda to solidify the false belief that I was abnormal.

Home Dynamics

At home, my family dynamic had not improved. I was jealous of my sister, Mel, a cheerleader who had many friends. I saw myself as fat and awkward, but she was always thin and popular. She had friends come for sleepovers, and guys would ask her out on dates for proms and dances. Her friends adored her. I was not so fortunate. She and I fought quite a bit over the years. I felt guilty and resentful and held grudges against her. And although my young brother and I had a friendly relationship, he mostly hung out with friends his age.

A Touch of the Spirit

I met a friend, Natalie, through one of the Synod events in the Lutheran youth group I attended. Natalie quickly became my best friend throughout high school. We enjoyed just being silly together. My sister became a youth leader that year, so all three of us traveled with a group to a conference held in Troy, New York. One of the women speakers at the meeting spoke so strongly by the power of the Holy Spirit that everyone was deeply affected. My sister and I were both sobbing as we acknowledged each other's pain. We felt drawn together by the trauma of our family dysfunction without being able to voice it. I hold that memory very dear to this day.

Additional Doses of Adversity

My junior year began with even more tribulation. Field hockey is supposed to provide an opportunity for players to encourage each other and to improve player skills. One day at practice, the coach decided that some of us should play on the junior-high team (composed of new-comers and sophomores), rather than on the varsity team. The coach demoted me and several others to the junior-high team. I was devastated, and shame and unworthiness filled my heart once again. Some classmates were furious over the unfair treatment and quit, but this had the opposite effect on me. I continued to play and served as a substitute for the varsity games. I also tried out for soccer that year. To my surprise, Coach Doc asked me to play defense on the varsity team. Playing soccer revealed my true love for running. The coach was supportive and caring. Many of the girls already had well-developed footwork skills, and I worked hard to catch up with them. I learned a lot about soccer that year and got in much better shape physically. I was so thankful to be part of the varsity team. Even though I was friendly with the other girls, I never felt like I was part of the group. That was disappointing, but today I realize how *discouragement shaped my identity.*

Vision for the Future

My faith in God increased along with my interest in reading the Bible. I began to read more, and the words began to shape my values and belief system. I strongly desired to stay sexually pure until marriage. This issue was important to God, and I knew waiting would enhance my relationship with my future husband. When I went out to eat with friends from youth group, we would talk about upcoming plans for college, waiting until marriage for sex, and avoiding alcohol.

We went on late night outings at a local diner where I would have a grilled, buttered blueberry muffin with hot chocolate. My friends and I would go cruising up and down Highway 145 in the evenings, looking to race with someone. We spent hours mindlessly racing around town. I chuckle when I think of that today. We would also drive by the houses of guys we liked. That was borderline-stalking, but today I think of it as being nosy and goofy. When I reminisce with those friends, we laugh at our antics as teenage girls with raging hormones.

The Race to the Date for Prom

Spring meant prom season! I was so excited and hopeful that a handsome classmate would ask me to accompany him. This hope was part of my fantasy of being seen, loved, and wanted. Of course, events didn't happen that way. I had a friend, Johnston, who was friendly, fun, and safe for me. He had a heart of gold and a love for Jesus. I was going to ask him to be my prom date, but another friend, Jael, beat me to it. I was sad, but I moved on. I ended up asking one of Johnston's friends, Don, instead, and we went as a foursome with Johnston and Jael. That year, I was also part of the county chorus and county band outside of my school activities. All of these activities truly gave me hope and saved my sanity by distracting me from tormenting, disturbing thoughts. At home, I was still dealing with my father's yelling or some other type of emotional abuse and the threat of physical abuse daily.

A Trip to New Orleans

I was so delighted to travel to a summer convention in New Orleans with the youth group. We converged on the New Orleans football stadium with over 25,000 other youth for Jesus Christ! We stayed at a local hotel, toured the city, and dined at Emeril's famous restaurant, per Johnston's request. The stadium experience was exhilarating! I remember singing one of my favorite songs, *"You came from heaven to earth to show the way, from the earth to the cross, my debt to pay, from the cross to the grave, from the grave to the sky, Lord, I lift your name on high!"* We all received a Bible at the conference. There was a Scripture on the back: *"And the Spirit and the bride say, Come. And let him that heareth say, Come."*[1] I often looked at the back cover of my Bible and wondered about what it could mean. Decades later, I finally began to understand this was Jesus Christ's invitation to me to accept Him as my Living Water, my hope, my sustenance, my safety, my everything. Jesus Christ longed for daily fellowship with me. I was so hungry and thirsty to know God better, but I always had a performance mentality blocking me from true intimacy and acceptance of what He did on the cross. But in that moment, I felt the Lord's presence, and I wanted to do the morally-right-thing daily.

One wonderful memory from this trip was our gathering at Café Du Monde at midnight. We saw a mime per-

---

1. Revelation 22:17, KJV

form and enjoyed hot coffee with a beignet (French pastry) while we lounged on that warm summer evening. This experience was a pleasant end to our time there.

The next day, some of us missed our flight. We got separated from the rest of the group and missed the boarding call. But the airline had overbooked the flight anyway, so they gave us a free room at a nearby hotel. The best part of it all was that I got bumped to first class on the flight home! I had no idea how wonderful it would be to sit in a roomy seat upfront and feast on fancy foods. That was an incredible experience! Today I would call it God's favor. That was my first time flying first class. I said to myself I wouldn't mind doing that again, but I would not have the opportunity until much later.

Double Work, Double Trouble

I was working mornings at a local daycare, but I got another job working the late afternoon shift at Dorney Park the summer before my senior year. I submitted my application too late to become a lifeguard, but I accepted a job as a "sweeperette"; the name says it all. I looked almost like a bumblebee (but without the black stripes) in my bright yellow overalls, white shirt, and white shoes and socks. The job was easy, sweeping up any trash or cigarette butts despite the discomfort of walking around in the hot sun. In retrospect, I could have saved a lot from these jobs. I am not sure to this day what I did with all that money.

Senior year was exceedingly busy for me. I played left half-back on the field hockey team. The need to prove myself was in full swing. I didn't join the marching band this year but maintained my position in the concert band and county band. That fall, I tried out for *Jesus Christ Superstar* and was cast as one of the 12 disciples. I had no idea how much Papa God would speak to me throughout this theater production. I loved the storyline of this play. I was deeply touched and would weep at times while I was in-character during rehearsals. The main events in the play actually occurred in history. I could imagine how Jesus would have felt when no one stayed awake to watch and pray with him and how he must have felt when Judas betrayed him. I had little idea about what God was doing in my heart during this show, but I cried over it for weeks afterward. God was calling me, yet I hadn't drawn very close to Him. He seemed far away, yet I was intrigued about the mystery of Him. Years later, God reminded me of this play and spoke to me about His purpose for me, as I recognized His call on my life during this time. God is so good!

During my senior year, my sister also played field hockey as a freshman. Participating in the same sport allowed us to hang out a lot together. My sister was great at field hockey and sports in general. She was on the junior high team at the same time I was on the junior varsity team. I sometimes played on the varsity team. This situation did not help my self-esteem or belief about my worth, but I still loved practicing for field hockey and running, thanks to soccer. I was also looking forward to all of the senior year events.

College Exploration

I applied to several universities in Pennsylvania and visited some of the campuses. My opportunity for a new adventure was near, and my enthusiasm was high! I had never received attention from my peers in high school. Their perception of me was inaccurate, but I had never felt free to show my true personality. I visited Kutztown University campus, which was okay, but I wasn't impressed with the atmosphere there. During the tour, I accidentally opened a door clearly marked as an emergency exit. Suddenly, the fire alarm went off, and everyone had to evacuate the building. This event was just one of many bloopers I have experienced in my life. I am sure the color of my face changed through every shade of pink and red.

Ten Percent of My College Decision

At beautiful Millersville University, as we toured the buildings, my heart fluttered with an inner suspicion that this might be my college. When we parked near the campus pond with the swans and the gorgeous landscaping, I felt even more sure about the place. But when we watched part of a baseball game going on that day, I realized that part of my decision to attend Millersville rested on other scenery: the handsome baseball players! I am not joking.

Later, my parents and I went to lunch in the cafeteria. While I was trying to show them where the trays were stacked, I accidentally hit a very handsome baseball player in the groin! I was so embarrassed. Fortunately, I did not know him and went on my way. I was thrilled to know what college I would be attending!

Numbing A Broken Heart

I loved attending high school football and braved the elements of nature to do so. Once during a game, one of the band members shouted out that I had a crush on one of the football players, announcing it in front of the whole student section! My face once again turned all the shades of red and pink imaginable. My heart was devastated once again. Surprisingly, some classmates invited me to join them for lunch in the cafeteria following this event. I do not know why I accepted. I had never learned to confront people who raged at my heart. My very disposition seemed to invite scorn, disrespect, and bullying. I had not yet learned to teach people how to treat me; that was still a distant lesson. I thought I had to bear with disrespect and harsh words at home, at school, and in the community. I was emotionally numb and did not realize how strongly the victim mentality held sway over my thinking.

No One Knows Me

My classmates did not really know me; they voted me as the shyest person. Today, my friends and family are quite surprised to hear that, because I am so confident and free now. However, at that time, I didn't have many deep friendships and often would eat in the home economics room because it felt like a safe space. Mrs. D. was kind and warm, and there were a few of us that spent time with her talking and laughing rather than being in the large cafeteria. I felt frustrated to be labeled the shyest person in the class because that was not my true self. I didn't want to be limited by other people's opinions. As I spoke on the platform at graduation, I imagined that I would be speaking in public later in my life. *The girl who felt boxed-in as "quiet, shy, and unknown" just wanted to scream out, "I have a voice, and my voice matters!"* However, the ability to convey that declaration remained hidden deep down inside.

A New Way of Life

Attending M.U. to study education was one of the best God-ordered decisions of my life. Although a bright student, I had lower SAT scores due to test anxiety, second-guessing, and overthinking my answers. I was 38th out of 142 in my class, most likely due to my insecurity with math courses. Because I had lower SAT scores, I received an offer to enroll in the PACE program to start my freshman year. This program was for students who needed a slower academic start to college. I was willing to enroll in this program because I wanted to go to Millersville so very much. I had hoped to stay in the co-educational dorms, but I was dismayed when I had to stay in the girls only dorms. Then I found out too late that I didn't need to participate in the PACE program after all. Through this circumstance, I met my roommate, Amy, along with her mother, and we spent the day together at orientation. I am thankful that Papa God directed my steps to Millersville, and I know He had a good plan for my safety. Amy turned out to be a trusted friend whom I call 'my rock' to this day.

My mom was sad, but I was very much looking forward to moving away from home and into the dorm. That first night at school marked the beginning of my ability to sleep without hiding fearfully under a blanket. This development was a welcome change. We weren't even using blankets at that point because the room was very warm those first few days.

Amy was a quiet, well-organized, and focused person. I, on the other hand, must have tried her patience with my piles of laundry and very creative organization patterns. My organizational skills have come a long way since then. Amy and I would talk a great deal at night, often laughing hysterically. She was learning Chinese, and we would hoot with laughter when we listened to the audio language tapes.

Amy introduced me to her friends at Intervarsity, a campus ministry for Christians, and I started attending a local Lutheran Church as well. She also invited me to a religious meeting where the students raised their hands during worship, which made me nervous. I wondered whether I had stumbled upon a cult with an ending involving Kool-Aid. However, all of the students were kind. Sometimes, I would hang out with them and watch movies.

I made some other friends on campus, went to some parties, and mingled with various groups. Once I went to a party and a guy walked me home and then kissed me. That was a refreshing experience! I was so excited, but he never spoke to me again, although I would see him in class. He was recovering from a breakup with a girl that he ended up marrying years later. He was not my type, anyway. I did hang out with some other guys who I would talk with now and then. I promised myself I wouldn't drink alcohol during my freshman year, but I ended up getting drunk the night before the chorus concert. One uncomfortable fact of getting drunk is feeling out of control. I continued to have a drink occasionally when hanging out with friends that year, but I didn't drink often, and I was frequently the designated driver for others who drank a lot.

I was still struggling to establish healthy eating patterns and curb my weight gain. I did not realize at the time that my overeating was because I wanted to hide and protect myself. I hid my true self from view to avoid further pain. I was still wearing a huge virtual mask and keeping people at arm's length. I had not regained my voice yet. Even if I had, I wouldn't have known how to use it correctly.

The first year of school ushered in a huge shift in my social life. I was meeting new people and felt free to communicate my true personality. I worked out because I enjoyed the exercise, but I still had issues with food. I had trouble deciding whether to eat or not. However, the struggle was not too serious yet. I just wanted to be seen, valued, and loved.

An Awakening

When I went back home for the summer, I noticed a change in my attitude towards my dad, and he sensed my anger over his continual mistreatment of my family and me.

At MU, I had tasted freedom from shame, humiliation, fear, manipulation, and anger. Men at college usually treated me kindly and with dignity. At first, since I was not accustomed to being treated well, I sometimes allowed them to take a metaphorical punch at me. I felt unable to stand up for myself in those situations. I would think of a good comeback, but not until later, and then I would stew about it. This scenario didn't happen very often, but I wanted people to see me as a kind, loving, bubbly person who accepts treatment as a doormat. When a person has been a victim for so long, what else do they know? They don't know any different way to respond.

Another Year of Adventure

My sophomore year led to solid friendships that have stood the test of time. Some events led to healing, and other events led to more pain, but I gained valuable lessons in every circumstance. The first change in my sophomore year was the chance to live in a co-ed dorm. Gaige Hall was a dark brown residential hall near the building where I had classes. The year before, some friends recommended getting a room with a girl named Callie. Rooming with her was quite the adventure. Callie loved patchouli, a plant from the mint family that smelled like wet soil. Let me add that it also smells musky and is potent to the nose, in my opinion. I could not get used to it, but I spent that whole semester trying to do so. Our personalities differed, but looking back, I could see that we both just wanted to be accepted, loved, and adored. Callie did not respect boundaries and it was a challenging time trying to navigate living with this roommate.

Fortunately during this time, I saw an advertisement for a resident assistant job. I hurried to apply because this job sounded like something I wanted to do. I would have a room to myself, and the duties seemed easy to fulfill: monitor the hallway, be there at the entrance of the building a few times a week, check rooms for fire hazard materials, and ensure proper fire drills. I hoped I would get the job.

Responding to Previous Complex Trauma

One night, I got dressed up and went to a little get-together with friends. At the party, I drank lots of "jungle juice," a concoction made with an abundance of mixed alcohol. I was quite intoxicated, and I did something I have never done and would not do again. Late in the evening, I walked up to every single fraternity guy and shook their hand. I mean, really? Yes, yes, I did. However, alcohol is a depressant, so at some point, I broke down crying on the stairwell. My friend Melissa was nowhere to be found (I was usually making sure she was safe). Somehow, I ended up in a dark room with a guy I didn't know. Thank goodness all we did was kiss, and then he walked me back to my dorm. I was crying so hard I was barely able to walk home. And after we got back, I sat on the floor in the dorm hallway and kept right on crying. Fortunately, my next-door neighbor came over to see if I was alright. I let her know that I was not okay, and she told the guy I was with that she would take care of me. I was so grateful for her questions and concern; otherwise, I might have made some poor choices that night. I could not remember the name of the guy who walked me home. The crying showed I was hurting badly, but I ignored it once again, which was easier to do than allow myself to feel the pain so I could do something about it. My roommate was not there that night, which worked out for me. The next day, my neighbor tried to soothe my hangover by giving me soda and crackers. However, this treatment really didn't help at all, and I felt like I was on a boat ready to explode like a soda can that has been shaken all night. Fortunately, I drank water later, and all the symptoms cleared up.

An Escape to the Beach

That year, my friends and I took a trip to Wildwood Beach. The shore felt like a haven and place of rest for me. Cold as it was, I hurried to the beach so I could run into the waves. We had so much fun that evening. The next day, we explored the town and went to the Crab House. I tried to eat crab, but the poop in the crab grossed me out. Instead, I ate

$20 worth of vegetable soup, which was delicious! That evening, we had some drinks in the hotel room. As we talked, one girl told us how her boyfriend had been sexually abused as a child by his cousin, who was a few years older. She was angry with the cousin. Immediately, the shame of my trauma responses towards others crept up and showed its ugly head. I said nothing about the incident, fearing rejection, anger, and the possibility of being labeled a freak due to my own trauma response. I wanted to keep these friends. I felt overwhelmingly guilty and pondered this conversation for days and days. My heart was heavy and full of pain and deep sorrow.

Even the thought of relating anything about sexual abuse is risky because some people may not understand. This is why people usually do not admit sexual trauma, although it occurs all too often and brings deep, deep shame. Instead of shining a light on deep shame, people try to hide it; but, trying to shame or ignore it has caused nothing but immense grief and sorrow across family lines and within society.

A week after our beach trip, I interviewed for the resident assistant position and, to my surprise, I got the job. I was now the new resident assistant starting the spring semester. I am sure other people interviewed, but I was so glad to be chosen. God was already ordering my steps even then, but I had no clue. The residential hall staff recognized my leader-ship skills and abilities, and I took advantage of this time to learn additional people skills and participate in team-building activities. I was thrilled because this job also meant that I would be parting ways with Callie. She was a lovely person, but not the kind of roommate I needed long-term.

I very much enjoyed having a spacious room all to myself for the next three-plus years on the first floor of Gaige Hall. I enjoyed creating artwork for my hallway, and I designed and painted door decorations. I drew and painted frogs on poster paper because I was ready to "leap" into a new year! As corny as that sounds now, that season ushered in the release of my creative genius that I had locked away long ago! During that semester, I made friends with three women on the second floor. I would stop in to visit them during my rounds as an RA.

During this time, I developed a crush on a tall red-headed guy on that floor who was super goofy. He was essentially my opposite. There were quite a few tall, adorable guys on that floor! Their shenanigans always piqued my interest. They studied a diverse range of subjects, including technology, education, science, and English. I made sure to walk past their hallway and say hello. I would chat with them during my walking rounds of the hall or stop in the girls' wing for some chocolate. I was in my glory as a social butterfly, pausing to say hello to everyone in the entire building, which brought me joy. However, amid all this fraternizing, I became a social chameleon and kept my heart locked up in a safe. This meant that I would adapt my personality to the people that I hung out with at times. I avoided talking about deep subjects with people. I was still not fully able to be myself then.

One evening, I was on duty in the office when Mr. Redhead came in late (most likely after he had a couple of drinks) and flirted with me for a long time. He seemed like a 'bad-boy' type and, of course, I was interested. But many minutes went by before I realized that he was flirting with me. I had no reference point for flirting because I had spent years hiding and avoiding this kind of situation. After we said goodnight, I was totally hooked on his words. We started corresponding through Instant Messenger. We would flirt for a while, but then he sent a message that I didn't quite understand. I asked some other guy to interpret what was in Mr. Redhead's message (he had written, "I want you"). The guy looked at me and explained that the words were quite literal. Then I realized that guys are pretty explicit when they ask for sex. On the topic of sex, women think about it often, perhaps, but they have a lot of emotions. They want to talk about love first, and then they get in the mood. Men, however, appear to be wired to think of sex apart from emotions. They are quick on the trigger. This tendency may not apply to every man, but based on life experiences, I have not seen very much evidence to the contrary.

I did not realize it at the time, but I was drawn to emotionally unavailable men. Mr. Red-head and I were like oil and vinegar. I was so naive, I could not pick up on his advances. I would much rather fantasize and have a crush on someone instead of attempting to pursue an actual relationship! I was still flirting with him, until one day, I realized he was talking more to this other girl. Oh, it hurt my heart! I found out from a confidant (another tall, adorable guy on the first floor) that Mr. Redhead was indeed dating this other girl. But during that discussion, my confidant also revealed that he had a crush on me! Imagine that! I was so clueless. Evidently, many guys had a crush on me, and I had NO idea of it.

That summer, I was obsessed with losing weight. The rejection of Mr. Redhead was so difficult to bear. I began to wonder what was so great about him, after all. I cannot, for a moment, remember one primary character trait that stood out. Okay, fine, he was intelligent and funny. The only other point seemed to be that he was emotionally unavailable.

As a social chameleon, I ended up attracting some toxic people during college because I had destructive behaviors. Particularly with my eating habits, my emotions were always up and down. On the outside, I smiled at people, loved them, and laughed with them, but still kept them at arm's length. I was beginning to understand myself somewhat, but I couldn't quite apprehend the total picture of who I was in Jesus Christ. I continued to attend the Lutheran Student Movement and the church on Sundays. I often met with other groups on Sunday, such as the Catholic group. I was having a great time meeting different people and speaking about my faith. However, I was unaware that I kept my distance from Papa God as well. I was curious about Him but did not want Him to get too close.

The Unraveling of Physical Pain

I began drinking meal shakes to lose weight quickly by the end of the semester. When I went home from MU during the summer, something horrible happened. After a Tae Bo workout, my lower back flared up in tremendous pain. However, I downplayed the problem after the pain had subsided somewhat. However, on an errand for cat litter for our family pet, I gasped for air when I lifted the heavy bag; the intense pain in my back returned. I visited the family doctor that week, and he checked my back and ordered x-rays. As soon as he saw the x-rays, he sent me to the top neurosurgeon in the Lehigh Valley.

I was petrified. The neurosurgeon showed me the MRI-scan of the herniated disk in LS-51 in my lower back and several degenerative disks in my upper back. His next statement frightened me. He said that if the disk had bulged one-quarter inch to the left side of my back, I could have been paralyzed. Instead, it was pinching my right sciatic nerve. My treatment options were physical therapy, an epidural injection, or surgery. Given my age, I opted for physical therapy. I was in extreme pain and could hardly move that whole summer. When I would put my foot down to take a step, I felt the pain instantly scorching through the bottom of my foot to the top of my back. I was upset because I couldn't move around much for the sake of weight loss, but I was eating less because of the pain. Often at night, I was in so much agony I would wake up and fall to the ground sobbing because I couldn't move. I returned to Millersville for my junior year with the back-pain issue still unresolved. Sometimes after class, I would require five or ten minutes before I could stand up.

Physical Therapy Mishaps

My experience at the first physical therapy appointment was entirely unexpected and a bit disconcerting. After a quick introduction, the physical therapist had me lay on the table with my knees in a butterfly position. Next, he climbed up on top of my knees to help stretch my muscles. It was quite an awkward position, and I felt mortified to appear this way in the middle of a room full of people.

The physical therapist did his best to provide exercises other than the butterfly one to alleviate the pain. My back pain progressively worsened in the fall, and I finally opted to get a double epidural injection of cortisol in my back. It was a huge deal for me to get an injection at all because I often fainted at anything having to do with needles. In just a few hours, I was crying again, but this time with tears of joy because I could walk and move without the torturous pain! It was a miracle! I went for a run the next day. I feel such freedom when I run; it allows me to release the nervous energy from anxiety and escape the world for a while. I was so thankful to be pain-free! I began to work out again and eat well that semester.

Soon my back had healed significantly and was strong enough for me to begin a more strenuous workout program. There was an upcoming mini-triathlon comprised of a rowing machine, running, and biking. I tied for second place with another girl in a field of 85 participants. I was so thrilled! My comeback was a remarkable achievement after a season of so much agony.

ABCD Eating Habits

I changed my eating habits considerably, and I was losing weight. The main concern about weight loss is that I began to limit the varieties of food. There were weeks where I ate just a few different foods, or else I fasted and drank only water. I was trying to control my feelings and break my destructive food habits in the wrong way.

While people told me I looked great, my mind believed the opposite. I had a distorted body image and could not discern it. Externally, my body was changing, but internally, my feelings, emotions, and brokenness were locked in the deep places of my heart, and I glossed over the primary cause of my dysfunctional eating patterns.

My family was concerned when they saw me. The worst part of my eating disorder was when I started taking diet pills and laxatives to lose weight more quickly. I was harming myself with my poor eating habits and lack of knowledge about nutrition and metabolism. Perhaps I was sabotaging myself because I was afraid to come out of hiding and face my pain.

One day, a friend who was concerned about my rapid change in appearance insisted that I go to the dining hall to eat. He and his girlfriend invited me to join them there. When I said I was not going, they just stood there, waiting. I hesitated for a few minutes and then agreed to go. As we started on the way to the cafeteria, I wanted to turn around and run back to the dorm, but I kept walking with them. I began eating again because people were telling me I looked great, but that compliment always confused me.

The Struggle to Believe I Am Beautiful

I would often go out with friends on the weekends. Once, I walked to a party with two of my guy-friends. When I walked through the door, the entire group of guys froze, staring at me. They told me I was beautiful. I wanted to hide under a rock or find the nearest exit! I did not love or value myself, and I could not accept being called beautiful. Although I longed to hear that word spoken about me, I was afraid of it.

While I was at another party that week, a sexy, muscular guy walked in, wearing a cowboy hat. John reminded me of a former high school crush. While I was busy just being my high-energy self with my friends, he gravitated towards me, and after we talked a while, I gradually realized he was hitting on me. I could not believe he was so enthralled with me.

John and I ended up making out on the hard floor of the living room, with other people present. That's not my style, but I went with it. I seriously considered spending the night in his truck, but thankfully, I made a somewhat wiser decision.

He was sweet and charming the next morning as we talked at breakfast, and much to my surprise, he called me the next day to see how I was doing. I felt giddy with excitement that this man seemed interested in getting to know me. I was also terrified that he was planning to visit me later that week. I freaked out internally when someone informed me that he said he was eager to spend the night with me. I was nervous and fearful down to the core of my being. Why did I feel this way? Wasn't I hoping to be noticed, seen, and wanted?

He brought a single rose for each of the girls at the party, but he gave me a bouquet and a book called the *Blue Day Book*, which I saved and kept in my book library. That was one of the sweetest gestures a man has ever made toward me. My heart swooned. When John arrived, we hung out in my room while I did some homework. I avoided any type of intimacy with this man. I was angry that he wanted to be physically intimate with me, but I could not identify why that was an issue. We made out for a little while, but I kept my distance. He ended up staying overnight, but we didn't have sex. After he left the next morning, I spent the whole day thinking about him. I endured such conflicting emotions; I liked him very much, but I also wanted to run away and hide.

He invited me to have dinner with him and his mother later that week, but I declined. I was running scared in the opposite direction. I had done this once before with a guy I made out with at a bar. Ugh, I admit I was a runner! I called him the next night. I felt awful for refusing the date with him, but I also felt afraid. Even though he gave me flowers and gifts and was very loving, I repelled the very attention my heart desired most. Unsurprisingly, he was distant that next day and I never apologized for my response. I wanted to see him, but I was full of shame, guilt, and confusion.

Shortly after the failure of this potential relationship, I met a charming guy at a bar. He was a model. We went on a date, but he smiled way too much for me. I didn't understand my attitude. I desired a guy with a tough exterior, built like the rapper 50 Cent, but with a soft heart of sweetness. My expectations were all over the place. I looked healthier on the outside, but inwardly, I was a hot mess. I still did not know how to love myself.

All the while, I began to have an interest in my new friend Mr. Blue Eyes. That summer, Mr. Blue Eyes and two other friends stayed at the university. I moved into an apartment with two other girls, and the three of us would go dancing at the Chameleon Club on weekends. Being a chameleon at the time, I fit right in. I didn't drink too much, of course, because I didn't like feeling out of control. That summer, I worked as an apartment assistant for free rent, in addition to my day job at the YMCA and my evening job as a hostess at Olive Garden. After work, I hung out with my guy friends at their apartment or someone else's place. I was putting on weight again, which was terrible. The struggle was intense, but I was not yet dealing with the root issue below the surface of the eating disorder.

These events formed the background of my life while my adoration of Mr. Blue Eyes increased. Earlier in the year, I let him know that I liked him. He was kind and gentle in saying he wanted to remain friends. I would go sing karaoke with friends and stay up late, then get up early for work. I also ran around with three other girlfriends who lived nearby and worked with me at the YMCA. I loved those girls dearly.

Avoiding Problems

A few months into my job at the Olive Garden, one of the younger girls developed an attitude and started being disrespectful toward me. The situation intensified to the point where I decided to quit. I was so tired of working with this unpleasant girl. Because I didn't have the guts to resign in person, I wrote a letter telling my boss that I wanted to quit. I took it to the Olive Garden and walked out. The next day, my supervisor called and left a message. I was so fearful that I asked a friend to return the call, pretending to be me, and confirm with Olive Garden that I quit. I don't recommend this strategy, but that's what I did. I finished the semester working at the Y.

The Aftermath of Not Valuing Yourself

Near the end of the semester, my friends and I started going to a place downtown called *Cherry Jubilee*. One evening, I met a tall, handsome guy named Jay that worked as a chef there. He had brown eyes and hair, and we were close in age. He exuded an air of mystery, and his rough edges attracted me. A week later, my friend Rich had plans to go to the bar with me, but he ended up not going. I was very disappointed because I very much wanted to see Jay, the chef.

I ended up going by myself. I sat there, dressed to the nines, and then I saw Jay out in the bar room. We had some drinks and talked a while. After the bar closed, we went to his friend's house to have some more drinks. In hindsight, this was a terrible idea. He and his friend played some video games and smoked weed. After an hour or so, he walked me back to his house. On the way, he picked a flower off a tree and put it in my long, flowing brown hair. I was a hippie at heart. I smiled and blushed because it was a sweet gesture. But once back at his apartment, the rest was history. I willingly gave up what I valued the most to a man I did not know. I gave up what I will call my virginity, despite the earlier abuse. I don't want to count that. The condom broke, but I assured him it would be alright. I woke up the next morning in a strange room in bed with a strange man, which didn't make me happy. That was odd; I had felt okay about it the night before when I'd had a few drinks. But this night of fun resulted in a urinary tract infection. I headed to a planned parenthood site in a dilapidated building downtown to get checked out. I was nervous and afraid because the woman checking my vitals didn't inspire confidence like my gynecologist.

It was that summer, I started taking pills to lose weight. I also took laxatives and made myself throw up often, learning the technique from a magazine article. During class one day, I felt dizzy and then fainted. I visited the school nurse, and then called a friend to pick me up and take me to the E.R. I was frightened as I waited to hear the results from the doctor. They said I was very dehydrated and had a severe urinary tract infection. They advised me to take the next day off.

I was sad because I would miss the last few days at the school, and I would miss Senior Wednesday at my favorite bar, *The Village*. Jay was supposed to be there with other friends. When I got home, my roommate angrily asked me why I was taking those pills. I began to cry and told her I didn't know. I sadly spent the evening in my room. The next day, Jay informed me that he had ended up in a fight at the Village. Perhaps it was a good thing that I didn't go. I went nervously back to my student teacher mentor because I hadn't left the classroom bulletin board in its usual order.

When I arrived, I noticed she had rearranged it without making any comment. Worse yet, I went to the staff meeting that morning wearing mismatched socks, which was blatantly obvious because I sat in the front row. Despite all of this I still had a glorious week. I enjoyed the last few days with those YMCA students.

The Job Search Adventure

When the time came to find a teaching job, I looked for one out of state. The thought of remaining in Pennsylvania and moving on from the relationship with Mr. Blue Eyes seemed devastating. And sadly, my friend, Matt, told me that he felt like he only knew me on a surface level because I didn't share much personal information.

I went to a job fair in Lancaster. The line of people waiting to speak with representatives from the Lancaster School District was very long. As I strolled around the event, I met a lady from Arizona. She interviewed me and asked me to submit some additional paperwork. I completed the application and was offered a teaching position in Arizona. I was very excited about the prospects for a new adventure and a new location!

Graduation: A Bittersweet Transition

The week before graduation, I went to see Mr. Blue Eyes, and my friend, Ken, was there, too.

Earlier that year, Ken had said something very disrespectful toward me, but I didn't defend myself. Strangely, my other two guy friends just sat there without supporting me. At the time, I just stood there and took the verbal abuse, but I later replayed in my mind what I should have said. I was still feeling disappointed by my two guy friends' inaction. I didn't know how to respond with dignity and self-respect. I knew Mr. Blue Eyes had it in him to defend a woman because he had once saved a friend from being raped while she was at a party. He had known where to find her, and he kicked open the dorm room door to rescue her.

The next day, I prepared to celebrate my time at MU. The party included all of my proud family and my Pappy. He always cries at graduations because he is so proud of us. My Pappy did not graduate from high school, and I wonder if the ceremony reminds him of what he missed as a teenager.

There was a party following the MU graduation, and my one-night stand, Jay, was there, too. I did not see Mr. Blue Eyes or my friends that evening. I had seen Jay at a show with some of my friends a few weeks before graduation. He came over to say hello to me, and I gave him a quick kiss. I was so nervous, and he was supposed to be working. Later on, I went over to talk to him. I was wearing my favorite outfit, and his friend said I looked like the woman in the Disney film. I speculated that they meant Pocahontas, and they chuckled. It was his friend's way of saying I was hot. I did not talk with Jay for very long. He gave me a long, durable kiss before leaving. I knew deep down I would not see him again. I didn't know him very well. It was a short fling of passion, but it quickly fizzled out.

I invited my brother, sister, and all of my friends, including Mr. Blue Eyes, to the last party I held at my apartment. We had fun hanging out all day. Later in the evening, I became very emotional and broke down crying and hugging Mr. Blue Eyes. I had many conflicting emotions; I was so sad to leave Pennsylvania, but another part of me wanted to be on my way to new adventures. I was twenty-three years old and loved to party, but I also thought I was ready for a husband and children.

Silent No Longer

Chapter 3

Why have I allowed darkness as an identity?
Why can't I get out of this disparity?

Off Like A Wild Horse
Hoping to Win

Armed with my double major in education, I was ready now to travel cross country on my new adventure to be a teacher in Florence, Arizona. I was thrilled, but also scared. Bridget (a girl I met at MU) agreed to share an apartment with me in Arizona. She was excited about her own new adventure teaching at a school near my new location. I would be moving out there first because my school began in July.

My mom and dad took turns driving with me as we embarked on the three-day journey to AZ in my green Ford Escort. I really enjoyed the scenery as we rode along, except for Oklahoma, which looked okay but smelled like a huge pile of manure. My mind was racing; I felt like I was on an emotional roller coaster ride during the entire trip. I didn't realize that my parents' anxiety was influencing my thinking processes. As we approached the Arizona state line, the thoughts in my mind seemed to get louder and angrier. I am spiritually sensitive, but I didn't yet realize the intangible influence of different regions on me. I felt like I was losing my mind—but I said nothing.

The Painted Desert in Arizona was one of our first stops, and it was even more beautiful than the pictures. The desert colors looked like dollops of sherbet in blue, yellow, orange, and purple. I took some photos of the beautiful scenery, but they don't do it justice. I still carry those images in my memory as clearly as I did back then. The weather that day was unusually hot, 122 degrees, to be precise!

A few hours later, we neared the Grand Canyon. I was surprised at the cooler weather in Northern Arizona. The landscape reminded me of green Pennsylvania. I loved my home state, but I was looking forward to this new transition. We paused to take a brief look at the Grand Canyon. I wanted to hike some trails, but we were short of time. The next morning, as we started the final four-hour leg of the journey toward Florence, the car's air conditioner quit working. I loved the heat, so I didn't mind. My dad was broiling, however. He drove speedily with the windows down, hoping for the traffic lights to turn quickly. Oddly enough, we didn't stop to get the air conditioner fixed. As we arrived in Florence, I saw a sign that read, "Don't stop for Hitchhikers-Florence

Prison Ahead." I gulped inwardly but kept a calm exterior for my parents' sake. My mom always worried a lot, and I knew that she would be frightened because the state prison was nearby. This little town was smackdab between Phoenix (an hour north) and Tucson (roughly an hour south). Florence boasted an Italian restaurant on the outskirts of town, as well as some Mexican restaurants within walking distance of my new place.

We arrived at the walled apartment complex and met the manager, who was very sweet. My beautiful, reasonably-priced apartment had three bedrooms and pool access. My parents helped me purchase a bed and get everything else in order. I quickly realized at that point how crucial it is to have money put aside. I was so grateful that my generous parents helped with the expenses. We went to the Italian restaurant for dinner. My mom and I cried a lot that evening. She was tearful at the thought of her first child leaving home, and I wept because I would be much further away from my family.

New Teacher Orientation

In July 2003, I started teacher orientation. I deliberated about what would be the best outfit to wear on a hot summer day. I showed up for work that morning wearing beige stockings with a black skirt and a dress coat. I didn't realize that wearing pantyhose while walking outside in 125-degree heat would be disastrously uncomfortable. Several administrators from the district welcomed me as I entered the room. Following the morning session, the new staff members boarded a bus to take a tour of Florence. I was sweating by the time we returned to the new school building, which was a 20-minute commute from my apartment. My excitement increased as I received my assignment to work with second and fifth-grade students. I spent the first few weeks getting to know my students and the teachers I would be working with throughout the year.

My roommate arrived three weeks later for the start of her job. My school was in session year-round with frequent breaks. Bridget was a wonderful roommate who understood the transition from Pennsylvania to Arizona. We had to commute separately because our school districts were in opposite directions. However, we were able to spend time together in the evenings after school.

I was doing reasonably well and was able to connect with the students at the beginning, but all that wonderfulness disappeared midway through my first year. The fifth-grade teacher I had been co-teaching with sent in her resignation. She was pregnant and concerned about her health because the school had not followed all of the mandatory immunization procedures. I agreed to teach the fifth-grade class until they found a new teacher, but my decision to take on that extra responsibility mid-term was not one of my better decisions that year. My stress rose to an exceedingly high level. I loved the adorable students, but overseeing the special education caseload was enough in itself without taking on someone else's job.

The overall structure and makeup of the class presented some challenges, and some of the students had behavior problems. I soon realized my classroom management technique was less than stellar. The problem was fixable, but I was not sure how to go about doing that. The dire state of my organizational skills reflected my internal emotional disarray. Add to that situation the advent of my sister, who moved in with me the latter half of the year for approximately three months. She was devastated by a terrible breakup with a man she dated for a few years. Mel and I would go to dinner at the Italian restaurant on weekends.

By the end of the year, I felt like a failure and was on the brink of forsaking education. That first year did not go as planned, even though I thought I was knowledgeable and prepared. I realized I had so much more to learn about myself and other people.

As a second-year teacher, I became an inclusion specialist to support students with learning disabilities in our third and fourth-grade classrooms. The school also hired a new teacher named Jai to teach students with autism spectrum disorders (ASD). Little did I know that we would eventually become best friends as we weathered many storms and trials. I had the privilege of working with excellent colleagues that year. I was the co-teacher for the four classrooms, and

I enjoyed watching the other teachers' interactions with the students and observing the different teaching styles. I liked my caseload and the students. But mid-way through the year, another proposed change came my way. The principal informed me that the K-2 Lifeskills teacher had stepped down from her position, before asking me if I wanted to take over the classroom. I took a few days to think it over and eventually decided to take the position. I loved the students and wisely began to use the former teacher's routine and structure. My small classroom was for students with learning support needs and other students who had self-care needs. As I also worked with paraprofessionals, I learned many valuable lessons on how to interact with these support people. In retrospect, I should have spent more time listening to the paraprofessionals. If I had, I would have been more direct, firm, and kind, while also communicating my specific expectations of my colleagues amid our daily routines.

Friendships for a Lifetime

During my second year in AZ, I temporarily lived with my friend Melanie (one of my colleagues) after moving from my first apartment. Melanie's broken engagement led to our becoming close friends. Jai, Melanie, and I started going out to a few nightspots in downtown Phoenix, where we had so much fun.

On our first night going out to clubs in Tempe, I danced with one of the hottest surfer, hipsterstyle men that ever set foot on earth. One might think I am exaggerating, but I am not. I was extremely shy, but I had a great night dancing with him while wearing my leopard shoes. Molly, Jai, and I hung out during the week, too. This season was painful for us all as we tried to make sense of relationships and gain some maturity.

As close friends, we supported each other when we dated various men or had difficult moments. Jai, another friend, was pregnant and going through a major breakup. The hardest decision of her life was to leave the father of her baby. Jai and I became best friends despite our differences. I was tall, loud, and giggly, with long brown hair, Jai was short, quiet, and soft-spoken, with platinum blonde hair. I was unorganized and always on the go. She was highly organized, routine-oriented, and fierce. We would sometimes argue like sisters. Jai and I had some difficult conversations to address our conflicts, and I was learning to express my feelings when I was frustrated. My favorite memories of our time in Arizona were when we ran miles around the golf course, watched movies, and hung out while eating bean dip or Mexican food whenever possible.

Molly would come over, or we would visit her. One night, we went to a club in the early days when Molly was pregnant. On the way home, about 2 a.m., she got a craving for What-a-Burger, a famous chain restaurant. When we were ready to leave, she drove my car out of the parking lot, and it stalled right in the middle of the road. Fortunately, the road was clear of traffic in both directions. I was so frustrated and blamed her (in my head) for stopping for a dang burger! But this was not the issue; the car's alternator was not working. One of our neighbors graciously picked us up and took us home. The next day, Jai and I went to the garage to check on my car. The tow truck driver had told me to put the key to my car in the glove box but now the key was missing. I was not happy that I had to call a locksmith to make a new key. We spent the whole day waiting for the car repairs to be complete.

Second Year Teaching in Arizona

Working with several older paraprofessionals brought my insecurities to light. I loved them all, but I was not good at accepting criticism or admitting that I wasn't perfect. I was far from acknowledging my faults due to deep-seated self-doubt. I was passive-aggressive back then and didn't know how to express my feelings appropriately. One day, out of frustration, I put up a sign outside our classroom door saying, "smile and be kind." Once again, this was not a shining moment in my history. As I look back on that situation, that sign was not a helpful way to address negative thinking. I didn't get along with one of the teaching assistants; she would frequently argue with me about how to handle student behavior. I finally went crying to the principal in frustration.

He was a great principal, but he did not advocate for students with disabilities. I was not acting as an advocate for my students in the manner I would be today. For example, our classroom met in a small faculty lounge during the construction of the new building nearby. There were eight adults and nineteen students in the program, but the size of the room was not appropriate for the individualized needs of the students. If the principal was not willing to hold a kindergarten class in the lounge, then having students with disabilities in that small, confined space is not acceptable either.

Spiders and Cactus, Oh My!

I spent many Saturday afternoons in the classroom preparing for the upcoming week. Once, I was sitting at my desk, talking to my dad on the phone, when all of a sudden, I saw a mouse spider near my foot (I was wearing flipflops). Mouse spiders are the size of a baseball! And this mouse spider lived up to these measurements. I panicked, screamed, and bolted from the classroom. What a scary moment! Mouse spiders' venom makes people sick.

At this moment, I was reminded of an experience in math camp the year before. I was taking a stroll on a desert path with a colleague from the camp. I was wearing a beautiful sundress, happily walking along until I stumbled and accidentally smacked into the side of a tall, unfriendly cactus. My friend, Willard, kindly helped extract all the cactus needles from my skin. Cactus needles sometimes cause bleeding, as it did in my case. I do not recommend walking into a cactus. Ever.

This account leads to another story (do not mind my purposeful digression). Once when I was walking down the new school hall, the gym teacher saved me from walking into a black widow spider hanging in mid-air. I have many spider stories, but all have a blissful ending: I lived, and the spiders ran away without biting me. There are a plethora of such narratives in my history. All of these stories are worth a laugh, and they beg the question, "Did that just happen?"

Great Uncle Bill's Journey Home

I went home for the holidays in December. My heart was full of sadness since my Great Uncle Bill, whom I cherished, was ill with throat cancer. In former years, I spent several holidays at his house. I was heartbroken to learn that he wouldn't accept any visitors but his siblings. Uncle Bill fought in World War II and had been awarded the Purple Heart. He was shot in the chest during a battle, fell into a cold lake, and miraculously survived. He never married and was the calmest, gentlest, wisest, and most caring man I knew. Uncle Bill's home was a place of safety and peace. His words were few but meaningful. He learned from my great-grandfather to be a man of prayer, and he was a man of great integrity. He didn't put on airs and was a reliable man in every setting.

I returned to Arizona and spent the next few weeks crying and praying for him. I decided to write a thank-you note to Uncle Bill to let him know how important he was in my life. Nana Helman called and told me she read the note to him in the hospital. In the days that followed, I often wept at night and prayed for Uncle Bill.

One particular Saturday evening, I felt enormous grief thinking about Uncle Bill as I drove home from visiting friends. I wept for him all the way home. When I arrived home, I immediately went to bed (around 1 a.m.). As I lay there, I prayed for Jesus Christ to take Uncle Bill home to heaven. I saw Jesus in a vision (while I was awake), as He walked towards my uncle. As Jesus stood in front of him, I saw Bill take his last breath. I knew my parents would call me the next morning to tell me the sad news.

Indeed, my mom called me the next morning while I was teaching Sunday school. I told her I already knew Uncle Bill had passed away. In the next breath, my mom confirmed what I had seen with my own eyes in a different time zone. Mom told me that at the moment when I prayed for him in Arizona, Uncle Bill passed away in Pennsylvania. God showed me He answers prayers that are in alignment with His perfect will. I will never forget Uncle Bill and the impact of his life on mine. I was sorry to find out that his house did not remain in the family. I wish I could have found a way to buy it. I did inherit many of the family picture frames that hung on the wall. Uncle Bill's Purple Heart went to my cousin, who was in the Marines during Desert Storm. But none of those items could replace the presence of Uncle Bill.

During the season following Uncle Bill's death, I felt tormented and far from a peaceful place, mentally. I still carried heavy loads of guilt and condemnation; they rolled over me like boulders weighing me down. One evening just before bed, I asked the Holy Spirit to fill me and give me a peaceful mind. Amazingly, the next morning I woke up with my mind, heart, and soul filled with peace. I no longer heard the voices of pain. I felt FREE and sane. However, that evening, the fear returned at bedtime. The next morning, my roommate informed me that she had seen a demon with straggly hair walking through her room the night before. She felt paralyzed with fear and could not speak as it walked into her closet. And after making several attempts to speak, she was finally able to speak the name of Jesus! She spoke out the blood of Jesus Christ as God revealed this demon going down the hallway near my room just at the moment when I felt overwhelmed by guilt and shame. I knew nothing about demonization then; I was horrified that a demon had been walking in the house. We didn't mention the incident again. This event was my introduction to supernatural occurrences in the spirit realm.

Many Choices, One Path to Follow

During the next month, I began searching for guidance concerning the next steps in my life. I had seen a brochure about missionary work in Africa, and I remembered my strong desire to go there. Since my early teenage years, my thoughts were full, dreaming and crying for the children who were fleeing their homes because of militant armies. Maybe that was what I should pursue. I also considered continuing my education by getting either a master's degree or teaching in Pennsylvania. I was accepted in graduate school at Arizona State University, the University of Arizona, and Lehigh University in Pennsylvania. Around the same time, I was also offered a job in the Lancaster County School District. I could not believe I had so many options! This season was an overwhelming time of decision-making in my life. This process made me realize that too many choices often muddy the waters of perception. God knew my plan already, and He ordered my steps.

The deadline to make a decision was quickly approaching. I also waited for a reply from the Human Resources Department in the Lancaster County School District. For financial reasons, I planned to work full time while pursuing my master's degree. I was pleased to receive an offer for a supervisory position with a community-based residential home through the university. The work-study program would provide tuition reimbursement for all classes. This was incredible news! Although all my options seemed positive, I decided to attend Lehigh University as my next step.

Unwise Decisions Lead to Lessons

I finished out the school year in Arizona. In late spring, my friend Teresa and I went to a party where there were several Minor League baseball players in attendance. I met a man named Gram, and we ended up talking together all evening. After exchanging numbers, he invited me to a daytime pool party his team was hosting the following weekend. Through the next week, we talked on the phone and texted each other. I went shopping for the pool party. I chose a cute orange top with brown pants and new sunglasses for the occasion. Sadly, my roommate and other friends could not attend. I was so nervous to go alone to the pool party but thought it might be all right because many people would be there. I was wrong. Only four men, including Gram, were in view at the outdoor pool when I arrived. I felt uneasy but I headed over to the small circular pool. I wisely decided to keep my clothes on and just dip my feet in the small pool. I felt mortified to be the only woman there. Gram and the men were drinking and talking crudely. They spoke about women who were 'easy' and would give it up the first night. Then they were arrogantly boasting about all the women who got drunk and slept with them. I was not drinking alcohol and I can't believe I sat there listening to this disturbing talk for nearly hours. At some point, I had to go to the bathroom. None of the men lived at the apartment complex. Fortunately, a woman who was a resident there and began swimming in the pool. One of the guys jokingly suggested that I pee in the pool. I ignored his comment and walked over to the woman to ask her if I could use her restroom. I was so thankful that she said yes. I followed her to her apartment.

When I came back downstairs, the guys were getting out of the pool to go somewhere else. I felt relieved. Gram gave me the drinks he bought me that I didn't drink, and I left. When I got in my car, I became angry with myself for driving down to this place alone, even if the party was during the day. I was also upset because Gram lied to me about the pool party. Only his friends were there, without dates, and I would have felt awkward to get in the pool with all of them. This party was not my style!

Once I arrived back home, I drove to my favorite Mexican restaurant and ordered a burrito, ate it by myself, and then called my friends to tell them what happened. I am glad that nothing worse happened to me, but I suddenly realized something. I had allowed myself to be in a potentially dangerous situation just so that I could be with Gram. In retrospect, the return was not worth the risk. I am worthy of better treatment from any man than the behavior I had witnessed that afternoon.

Following this incident, one of the other teachers wanted me to date her son. I went on one date with him, weeks later, which was interesting. He picked me up at the house, but once we were on our way, he began to tell me about his time in counseling and blathered on about a wealth of depressing topics. Then he exhibited road rage while I was in the car with him. I appreciated his taking me kart racing and to dinner, but he disclosed too much personal information for a first date. There was no love connection. I was moving back to Pennsylvania soon, so that helped me be honest; I told him I was not interested in any future dates.

Transition Back to Pennsylvania

Jai and I worked long hours and had adjusted to the new schedule with the arrival of her precious little boy. I had a difficult time leaving my best friend and her little man. I cried as I held him on my last day in Arizona. We had gone through so much together. She is a sister and friend for life. Molly also celebrated along with me, my Mom, Dad, Teresa, and Jai. I spent my last weekend in Arizona at my favorite spot called Canyon Lake. The road had winding curves that I loved to drive down because there were no barriers or guard rails. I loved to cruise around that Canyon on any day instead of going through tunnels or on roads with high guard-rails.

My parents and I packed up my green Ford Escort and put the larger belongings in a U-Haul truck. If I had to do it over again, I would just take the essentials. This trip reminded me of the trip out to Arizona. I packed many teaching materials that later collected dust in my parents' attic for years.

Another sad moment was saying goodbye to my students and the paraprofessionals. I loved all of my students, but I had a soft spot in my heart for one student, Manuel. During the past few years, I was close to his family. I took him and his brother to the YMCA during the summer, and my staff and I bought bikes for them. I cried as I wrote my farewell letter.

Looking forward, I realized that my leadership skills needed attention. In Arizona, I learned a lot about working with colleagues (particularly paraprofessionals), but I had a lot of insecurities then. I was not very good at being direct in my communication. Today, I do a much better job of loving, listening, directing, and honoring people I work with professionally.

Back then, as a result of my deep wounds, I often misconstrued others' opinions of me. I tried to please everyone at the cost of my self-respect. One of my biggest mistakes was thinking that two of the kindest paraprofessionals I had were gossiping or slandering me. I gave them lower scores on their observation but never addressed any of my concerns. Unfortunately, my perceptions were not accurate, and I hurt them in the process. It was one of my earliest and most painful moments as a leader. Based on this initial misconception, I have since learned how to address situations skillfully with people and discuss my feelings. Those earlier experiences have shaped my ability to be a loving leader. Humility is truly the best leadership tool available for daily use.

Unraveling The Deeply Wounded Heart

In June 2008, my parents and I drove cross country back to Pennsylvania. I was sad to leave Arizona but excited for new adventures. I was now almost 27 years old. I decided to live with my parents while attending Lehigh University. My sister was still living at home, working locally, and my brother was home from college for the summer. Before leaving Arizona, I carried deep levels of condemnation and remorse over my darkest and most shameful sin that occurred as a child. I was tormented by ongoing flashbacks and tidbits of blocked memories from the time I was a little girl. Chains of bondage held me captive ever since I first felt condemnation as a child. I did not understand that I had learned these behaviors from other people who had sexually abused me.

Nonetheless, I had sinned sexually in my response to sexual trauma, and I wanted to acknowledge it. Before I traveled back to Pennsylvania, I decided to write a letter to my sister and mother, telling them that I needed to discuss something important with them. The contents of that letter alluded to some grievous news, so my mom and sister were wondering if I had a serious health problem.

Also, before leaving Arizona, I decided that when I got back home, I would confront Uncle Manwell (my dad's uncle) about the sexual abuse I experienced as a child. That was my first step to make sure I was not going crazy, inventing a scenario in my head about being abused. I had believed that I was sinful, dark, and filthy. I wanted to confirm that sexual abuse had made an impact on events in my life. My heart tried to believe that I was the problem and that I was the only one at fault so that the pain of sexual abuse would not sink in too deeply.

Confronting The Past

The week I arrived back home, I asked my grandfather for Manwell's phone number. He told me, to my dismay, that Manwell had moved to Virginia years ago with his wife. I was devastated and deeply discouraged by this news. I wanted to talk with him before I told the family about my notion of sexual abuse at his hands.

The next day, my pappy called me and told me that Manwell was in Pennsylvania visiting that week. God is amazing. The way He continued to orchestrate these healing events in my life was incredible. I dialed Manwell's number, and he answered, calling me "Mandy." I must have cringed a billion times over that nickname. I hated it. I asked him if he could come over to our house. I don't really know why I didn't just ask him to meet me somewhere. He and his brother Eddie both came over to visit. When Manwell came in, my brother Mark was sitting next to me, but he moved to a different seat. I was secretly screaming inside for my brother to stay next to me. I knew what would happen next. Manwell hugged me and then sat right next to me. This same man slapped my butt when I saw him at a family event when I was 12. Manwell and his brother visited with our family awhile, and then they left. I did not even get to touch the surface of what I needed to address with Manwell. I decided to call and ask him to meet me at a local diner for breakfast. He said yes, and he picked me up in his van the next morning. My intention for this meeting with Manwell was to help me figure out the truth about the darkness of my childhood. The results would be a critical factor in deciding whether I would check myself into a mental hospital. I do not say that lightly.

The next morning, Manwell greeted me as I climbed into the van. The 12-minute trip to the diner felt more like an hour's drive. We sat down, and I managed to order oatmeal, sitting across from a man who had possibly violated me as a child. I somehow was able to eat breakfast and listen to him joke about hiring me as a nurse at his home. His wife was not well back in Virginia. Of course, the idea of being a nurse in his house made me feel nauseous. As he talked, I tried to figure out a way to bring up the main conversational point, but I just could not find the words. I listened to him compliment me all the way home. When he parked the car, I knew I couldn't wait any longer. I said, "I feel like something bad happened to me when I was a child." That statement was all that I could muster. He paused and then answered, "Well, sometimes bad things happen, but you keep moving." I repeated my sentence and then was silent. I got out of the car and thanked him for breakfast. He reached into the back seat and gave me a stuffed teddy bear with "Somebody Loves you in Virginia" on it. I took it, and as I walked into the house, my dad was there yelling at me about something. I ignored him and ran upstairs to my bedroom. My body knew. The body always keeps score.[1] I realized that Manwell had sexually abused me as a child. My entire body shook as I wailed

---

1. Van der Kolk, 2014

and cried. There was no one to comfort me. I stood in front of my closet and wept. I did not realize that God had engineered this event to help me get free of immense condemnation and begin my deep healing journey. I felt more mentally sound at that moment, but the effect was temporary. My family knew I had gone to breakfast with Manwell even though it seemed odd. Manwell kept calling me all week and left messages on the house answering machine. I chose to ignore his calls. He even called my grandparents, which was so awkward because he was asking about me. I had finally confronted the man who I believed to be the only person to violate me sexually. I would find out more about my story over a decade later.

I spent a lot of time processing what had happened with Uncle Manwell. In the meantime, I still suffered heaps of condemnation about my response to sexual trauma as a little girl. I knew this conversation with my sister had to happen soon. Later that evening, no one else was at home, so my sister and I sat on the couch together in the living room. I revealed to her that I thought Uncle Manwell had sexually abused me. The tears started as I told her all about what he said and how my body knew. Then I confessed that because of this abuse, I wanted to apologize to her for anything I had done. I could not say the words and got all choked up. She knew what I meant and spoke the words, "touched her inappropriately," and I began weeping. When my sister hugged me and accepted my apology, I felt huge waves of forgiveness and freedom pour into me. As I kept weeping, something that felt like heavy cinder blocks of condemnation fell off my back. I was so sorry for what I had done. I had suffered from decades of self-condemnation. A long time later, I realized that the inappropriate touching started when I was past age seven, and it ended when I was nearly eight after I learned about "good touch" and "bad touch" in my second-grade classroom. Later, I told my brother about Uncle Manwell and the conversation with Mel.

When someone has experienced sexual trauma, they will most likely repeat what happened to them with someone of the same sex. They are reliving what happened, but they are not fully conscious of it. *Reenacting sexual trauma can begin early and most likely will continue into teenage years through adulthood if the emotions surrounding the events are not processed. Copying the initial abusive events can keep happening and may become part of a person's identity.*

My sister and brother agreed that I should tell my mom privately about Uncle Manwell's abuse. My dad would hear about the abuse later. When I told my mom about it, she said that she always watched us and couldn't remember a time when I was alone with him. However, I traveled with Uncle Manwell and my aunt and stayed overnight once at their house. I don't think my mom was able to be very aware of the situation because she was dealing with her own trauma and mental health issues, including domestic violence at the hands of my father. She was so sorry that it happened, and she was also angry. My mom cried in my presence as she often does if something is hurtful. I was distressed to see my mom so upset by this. My father and I don't have a very close relationship. When I told him about the sexual abuse, he did not offer any comment. He sat on the front porch and did not say a word. Years later, he claimed that I had not told him at all.

My general emotional state felt a little lighter after the revelation. During this time, I was searching for a church family that I could call home. I visited a few churches and then decided to attend Life Church in Allentown. I loved the worship music and the diverse crowd of people. God had called me here to continue my journey with Him. I sat in the middle of the auditorium on most Sundays, and I was minimally involved in church activities.

The Journey at Lehigh University

My Lehigh University coursework began at summer's end. I took part in training classes to become a full-time supervisor of a community-based program. I had no idea that I would soon meet three people who would change my life. Since I had some previous experience working in a community-based home at Millersville University, I was glad to be working with adults in the community once again.

One of the clients was autistic, another had Down Syndrome, and the third was a woman with an Intellectual Disability. All three of these amazing people had been in institutions where they either suffered abuse or had witnessed others' abuse. Since all three had limited speaking ability, they were unable to convey what they had seen, and the actual impact on their individual lives was largely unknown. However, some of the behaviors I observed, such as eating quickly, hiding gifts after opening them, staying silent, bursting into anger, or excessive self-protection such as wanting to remain in their room, are some tell-tale signs of trauma and abuse. These people lived at the community-based home for over two decades after the institutions had closed. A university grant supplied funds to support individuals in community-based residences, and students conducted quality-of-life research on how to support each client's independence. I enjoyed spending time with all three of our clients and intentionally made a personal connection with each one. I knew that this supervisor's job was a good fit for me.

During my first week of training, I met another supervisor, Dee, who was a lot of fun. We quickly became friends and spent time with other employees who worked at the community-based homes. She was in the counseling psychology master's program while I was getting my degree in Special Education.

I attended my first class at Lehigh on my 27th birthday. My course of study focused on inclusive practices for individuals with disabilities. I got to know several fellow students that I still talk with occasionally. I was anxious about how I could pursue my studies in addition to working full-time while I was still living at my parents' house. I had very little idea that this setup would be part of my healing journey, but God knew it.

I was having so much fun hanging out with my new friends Dee, Jess, Jen, and Megan. One night, Dee and I spent the whole evening at a favorite local bar and managed to get home in the early morning. I valued my friendship with Dee. We had similar family issues, but our different areas of strength complemented each other, bringing balance to the relationship. I was still trying to figure out how to handle the combination of school-work and my supervisor's job. Four months into the position, my anxiety was getting intense because living with my parents was becoming more challenging than ever before.

Time to Move Out

One night when I was at home, my dad had an explosively angry outburst because I forgot to fill up the Brita water-filter pitcher. He violently lunged toward me, but my brother stepped in between us. He didn't say anything to my dad, but he glared threateningly at him. This action dismantled my dad's power trip. I cried later that evening because I knew I could stay no longer at the house. My father had always had outbursts of temper. My siblings and I grew up in this toxic environment, laced with his constant verbal assaults. He shouted to assert his power and control. In short, the whole situation was exhausting, but at that moment, I realized that I didn't have to put up with it anymore! That night, I thanked my brother for being there for me.

Sometimes I wondered why my mom stayed with my dad all those years. I was angry with her for remaining with him, and I couldn't comprehend what dynamics kept her there. I now understand that fear is the primary factor that keeps people trapped in ongoing abusive relationships. Staying with a man who continually threatens, degrades, punishes, and demeans is probably an endless nightmare. I lived in this scenario, too, but I played a different role. Now my tolerance for this abusive and hostile environment had run out. I carried a lot of suppressed rage, but I needed more revelation. My pain was stewing deep down inside me to the core of my being.

I suppose I could have taken out a loan and rented an apartment, but that thought didn't occur to me. The idea that I was unworthy to obtain an apartment kept me from believing the truth: that getting the apartment would have been a healthy decision. I was operating under a poverty mindset, generously sprinkled with fear of the unknown. I decided to relinquish the supervisor's job and request the position of an overnight intern, who would be living on the third floor of the home. My transition to the overnight intern hours went well.

Chapter 4

Why does fear, shame, and guilt surround me?
Why can't I just be free?

Relationship Decisions

About six months later, Dee and I were out at a local dance club when I met my first actual boyfriend, Tony. Tony, of Haitian descent, was nine years older than I. I love dating men from diverse cultures. After an enjoyable night of dancing, Tony asked for my number and called me the next day. We talked for hours, and then he asked me to go on a date. Wow! This was my first date that led to an actual relationship. We went to a local café for dinner. Tony told me about his eight-year-old daughter, whom he visited on weekends. After dinner, we hung out and then went to his apartment. At first, I didn't think anything of the low light levels in his apartment. Then I noticed the inflatable mattress on the floor in the living room. I stayed there with him for the evening. In the following days, we began to talk and hang out almost every day. We went on more dates, and then he stayed overnight at my apartment for the first time. During the night, I saw in my dreams a demon I had never seen before. The dream's images rattled me, but I did not understand what it meant. Tony and I became official as a couple after a few months of dating. This was the first time my family met a man I was dating. The meeting with my parents went well overall, but it was more challenging with my racist grandparents.

After a few more months, Tony moved in with me. I thought this was a good idea at the time, but Tony seemed to be suffering from some kind of personality disorder. I did not recognize this at first, but gradually I began to notice that when he got upset, he would become furious, and that scared me. Other times, though, Tony would calm down and pretend to be an angel. But at one point, he yelled at me when we were sitting in his car one evening, and I became so afraid that I got out and walked the city streets in the bitter cold. Tony tried to find me, but I just kept walking; I was so sad and full of grief. He had spent several holidays with our family, and my mom had invited his daughter for dinner several times. But the whole time, I was conflicted about sleeping with him because my goal was to wait for marriage. Sex before marriage wasn't part of my core values, and I was ignoring my belief system.

Tony was there for me, however, when I went through some hardship, and I appreciated what I gained from the relationship. One thing I did learn was how to navigate difficult conversations about racial tension. I had to tell my grandmother before Thanksgiving that Tony might not want to come to her home. When she asked why I told her he did not feel welcomed by her. Amazingly, my grandmother's attitude shifted, and he joined us on Thanksgiving. I often thought that Tony would ask me to marry him. I earnestly desired to be married, but deep down, I knew he was not the one God had for me.

Wedding Season Mixed with Bridezilla

I participated in several weddings that year, but Tony only attended one of them with me. I tried for a year and a half to make this relationship work. For one thing, I was so frustrated over trying to share one car with Tony because his car had caught on fire. We had a major disagreement over this situation. I met his mother in New York City one weekend, but he would not go into the church with us during our weekend visit. I went anyway because it was important to me. Tony had a lot of problems. In particular, he carried a lot of guilt about the childhood loss of his father. The last few times I saw him, he was verbally abusive toward me. I was used to mistreatment and believed that I deserved it. One time he called, saying that he could see me through the windows. Fortunately, that wasn't true, but the incident left me unsettled. We ended the relationship just after the Christmas holiday in 2008. I wept heartbrokenly following the breakup with Tony. I felt so lonely, even though I realized our relationship wasn't healthy in the long term. Later on, I was thankful that God had helped end it.

A Harrowing Experience

I was also a bridesmaid for my friend Allison's wedding in October. I loved the red dress I wore and was thrilled for her. Ali and I had been friends since grade school, so my whole family went to the wedding. My dad had been drinking a lot, and toward the end of the evening, my mom and brother took him home. I had gone to my friend Rachel's house after the reception. While I was talking with her, I received an alarming phone call from my mom. After they got home, my still-extremely-intoxicated dad had gone upstairs when my mom and brother heard a loud thump. They both ran upstairs to find my dad lying on the floor with a gun on top of him. My brother was distraught and rushed over to him. My dad woke up then, but he was severely ill. He told them he had been snorting cocaine and drinking all night. He said that he felt like he had literally died and come back to life. He then threw up all over the carpet. When I lived in Arizona, my mom and brother had experienced my dad throwing up all over the house, so I escaped the trauma of witnessing that scene repeated. My father never explained why the gun fell on top of him. He was very weak that evening.

I rushed over to the house. While my dad was on the floor, I said a prayer with him, and he got up from the floor and went to his bed. His cousin, Ronnie, and Ronnie's wife, Paulette (she's a nurse) came over to the house to check on him. Paulette only stayed there for an hour since it was late in the evening. We didn't call 911 because we knew my dad would lose his job. We just sat there with him for a long time. During this whole drama, I did not give in to my emotions. I took the leadership role of making sure everyone else was cared for, and then I went to sleep. My dad had mocked me in the past few years whenever I talked about God, but now he was in a hard place. I prayed for him often during this time. That week, my dad agreed to quit using cocaine. He only used once more that following week, and then he decided to go to a Narcotics Anonymous meeting.

One particular night that week, my dad drove to an NA meeting which met in a local church building several times a week. Finally, he got up the courage to go inside. My dad was able to quit cocaine with the help of God and the support of this group. He was extremely thankful and became close with the Lord God once again. God had saved my dad from death. **God has a way of protecting us from death and destruction, no matter how hard we try to destroy ourselves, especially when someone continually prays for us.**

A week later, my dad told me a story about temptation and testing of heart. One day at his workplace, a dealer was at the bathroom door. But, God is faithful. My dad knelt on the bathroom floor and prayed for help. He said he was sweating very badly and felt like he spent an eternity on the floor. Fortunately, the man at the bathroom left, and my dad stood firm in his faith to stay away from drugs. He turned aside and prayed to his power source—Lord God. The dealer never approached my dad to offer drugs again, and my dad overcame this strong addiction.

No matter what the focus of the addiction is, those caught in it try to alleviate their symptoms without resolving the root issues. Addiction isn't only to substances (food, drugs, alcohol), but also certain behaviors (gambling, shopping, sex). *Addiction is rooted in abandonment, rejection, and a lack of love, first from God, and then from others.* Addicts are deeply wounded people, who sometimes unknowingly blame God for their problems. They don't realize that their destructive, prideful choices stem from mistaken ideas about who God is and their identity in Him.

My relationship with my dad changed at this point. I could now talk with him about God. My dad tried going to counseling, but he was not ready for it. His defense mechanism was to always joke and find humor to deflect acknowledgment of the more profound healing that was needed. My dad seemed to think he could convince people he was doing well just by putting a good face on his situation. Despite this, Dad continued to recover and remain in NA. However, he did not get to the main root of his problems.

People often may not know how to delve deep into their healing, or they lack the courage to take off the mask they hide behind. The most dangerous lie people tell themselves is that acknowledging their pain will be too much trouble to be worth the effort. They don't understand that courageously facing the pain and dealing with the roots of it will actually free them up and propel them forward. If the deepest root of addiction is not uncovered and resolved, other addictions may arise and deflect attention from the core issue. And the truth about that deepest root always comes to the surface at different points, even if people don't recognize it.

We planned a big surprise party for Dad. Many of his close friends and family were on the guest list. His mother, my other Nana, also attended. I was not close to her. She was not partial to my dad, and we were not her favored grandchildren. When I was little, I couldn't understand why she didn't invite us to visit her as she did the other grandchildren. I don't know if she ever acknowledged this favoritism or felt guilty about it. Nana eventually had a major stroke, which put her in the hospital, dying. I went to visit her one last time and prayed with her. I didn't tell her that I forgave her for rejecting, abandoning, and not giving me the love I needed. I told her I loved her because I realized that she didn't know how to love me, but she did her best. Years later, I now understand that she was in an abusive relationship with a man who demeaned her the same way my dad treats my mom. ***Generational patterns that lead to profound abuse of self and others are preventable. If the victims of abuse sought healing of their deep wounds, they could break the cycle of destructive behavior patterns.*** They can choose to learn how to pursue healing on a deeper level, learning how to receive love and then love others. No one can give something they do not possess; therefore, a close relationship with Papa God is paramount. He is the Source they can depend on to help them navigate the whole process of healing.

A New Transition

In May 2008, I was six months away from graduating with my Master's degree in Special Education. I took a course for additional certification to teach English learners (ELs) or people who are learning English as a second language. The professor of this course encouraged me to take my GRE (Graduate Record Examinations) and get my doctoral degree. He told me I was brilliant and that I could gain acceptance into several universities, including Harvard. His encouragement meant the world to me because he was a brilliant man who I greatly respected.

My applications for university doctoral programs were due mid-February at Lehigh. My friend, Dee, also applied for the same degree. I had extreme test-anxiety all through school, but I took the GRE in January without any preparation. Early into the test, I sensed that I was not doing well in the math portion. My anxiety levels skyrocketed through the remainder of the exam. I suspected that I would have low scores, and I did, but it was mostly due to the math portion. I applied to several universities despite this fact. A few weeks later, I interviewed with Lehigh University. Some faculty members had questions about my GRE results, but I was honest and explained my grades in the master's program. Weeks later, I received a letter of acceptance into the Ph.D. program at Lehigh University! I didn't get accepted by two other universities, which I attributed to the low GRE math score.

I felt strangely indifferent and almost sad after I received my Ph.D. acceptance. There were several reasons for this. Some element seemed to be missing in my life. People (including some people I just met) were encouraging me in my counseling skills, but I felt unqualified. I didn't feel confident that I had anything to offer as a counselor. Additionally, the latter part of the master's program had been stressful and led to additional weight gain. Throughout the master's program, I was working out, sometimes at 6 a.m. with Dee, but food still represented comfort, safety, and support. Food kept me feeling hidden and secure from unsafe people and environments. Subconsciously, I convinced myself that hiding was better than risking sexual violation.

Finally, I was unaware of my lack of emotional stability, particularly regarding relationships. Following the breakup with Tony, I was not able to handle any relationship. Despite that, in the first year of the doctoral program, I began talking to several men. I went out with one guy who was in a different graduate program at Lehigh. I was also friendly with another man who was a Jehovah's Witness. Then I met a third man at the local music festival near the end of the summer. We spoke on the phone the next day at great length, but he was going through a separation from his girlfriend, so we did not talk again for months.

One weekend, our graduate study group had a Halloween Happy Hour. I heard a tip about free beer for the first 300 people attending the party. That night I went as Sarah Palin. I wore fake bangs and a black suit decorated with her obnoxious quotes on post-it notes. Later in the evening, my friend Jen and her husband set me up to meet his tall Greek co-worker, Theo. Wow. He made a grand entrance into the bar wearing a devil costume. I took one glance at him and knew I was in trouble. He was exceptionally handsome. We all had some drinks, but I had way too many. Later, I took Theo by the hand and led him outside to make out with him. That first kiss was awkward because I was not sure what he was trying to do. I felt like he was possibly trying to break off my teeth. Then we all went back to Jen's house. Theo invited me over for lunch the next day. I made some poor decisions on that lunch date.

Jazzercising My Way Through Life

I loved my aerobics class. Dee and I attended Jazzercise twice weekly with other energetic grad students. One of my favorite dance *moves*, "wash-the-car," made me feel like I was in the movie, *The Karate Kid*. That class was a rejuvenating oasis between some long days working in the community-based homes. We laughed our way through the class, our giggles punctuated by my frequent but strategic checks of 'Hot Owen' in the mirror, another crush I had. I kid you not, while I was in my exercise class, I could see him in the other room due to the mirrors. He'd have his shirt off, his impeccable "you-could-fry-an-egg-on-these" pecs and abs on display. Hot Owen lived in the apartment house beside mine. Once, I boldly asked one of the men I worked with to walk up the block with me because Owen was walking home, and I wanted to walk past him. But I never spoke to him.

In October, I renewed my friendship with Derk, the man I'd met earlier at a music festival. We spent hours, once again, talking on the phone. While I was on the way to a restaurant Friday evening with Theo, I was making a date with Derk for the next day. (Yes, my behavior was disgraceful.) I was also texting my Jehovah's Witness friend, who was going to hang out with me later that night.

On Saturday, Derk and I headed to Philly. We had a good conversation during the car ride, stopped for lunch at a burrito spot, and then spent time walking around the town. Before we got home, he kissed me. The next day, he texted me that he had decided to go back with his wife he had separated from that summer. Wait; what? I was in shock! I had no idea his 'separation' was, in truth, a break with his *wife*, not his girlfriend! I texted him to wish him well, and then I spent hours crying on the sofa. I had felt a more personal connection with him than all the men I was spending time with that week. The next evening, Derk texted me again, saying he thought of me as he watched our favorite football team. I could not believe this man was still trying to keep in touch with me! I told him that we both knew it would be wrong to continue our association and that he should go back to his wife. I told him not to text me again. That was the end of that relationship.

I was a hot mess. I was still dating my Greek friend, Theo, but he was emotionally unavailable. He told me to let him know if I began to get feelings for him. One day after he was with me at a picnic, he dropped me off at my friend's bridal shower. I texted him later that night after I got home, and he came over in the wee hours of the morning. The next day I texted him, telling him that I would have to stop seeing him because I had fallen for him. I was so upset. He did not respond for over a week because he said he lost his cell phone. When he did respond, he thanked me for letting him know. In the wake of that loss, I briefly dated a man from India whom I had met at my friend's wedding reception.

Upcoming Changes

At the end of the first doctoral year, I left my community-based internship to become a Transition Coordinator. I was so nervous about getting an apartment that I settled for a situation that would lead to a more significant deterioration of my overall health. If I hadn't been so afraid, I could have looked into renting a house or apartment. Instead, I decided to live with two clients from the new program, men with disabilities. One man was autistic, and his roommate had mental health concerns. I thought I had enough experience to manage this type of living arrangement in the upstairs apartment. I also thought it was a great idea to adopt three little cats from the street. Mimi was an adorable stray female cat who often came to the door of the group home. I just fell in love with her. My friend Jess would have had her spayed, but we soon found out that Mimi had recently had three little kittens. In April, some neighbors, wearing gloves, repeatedly tried to collect the little ones that were nursing with the momma cat, but they did not have much success. Mimi felt safe with us but not with them and would hiss and scratch as she tried to protect her little kittens. My plan to save all of the kittens failed. However, I did get the momma cat (Mimi) and one kitten, who I decided to call Cici (from Cecelia).

I would let Mimi out to feed the other kittens daily. I thought Cici was a girl until later when my friend Jess told me it was a boy! Later on, I also adopted another little cat who I found outside the apartment alone. I was a vegan humanist then, with a soft heart for animals in general and cats in particular. I love cats but did not do a great job at training them around the apartment. I have now decided that these cats probably will be the last animals I steward as an official owner. I haven't been very organized most of my life. I didn't love, value, or cherish myself or my belongings. Honestly, I barely felt alive and in the present. That was a particularly confusing time in my life.

Transitioning to a New Career Position

In July, I moved to my room in the new apartment at the Community Living home. The place didn't have a kitchen and was on the third floor. In retrospect, I realize I made that choice out of fear rather than confidence. The rent was also more expensive than it should have been. My cats found the new place enjoyable, but I had to go through the house to get to my room. This inconvenience was another reason to try to bargain for cheaper rent without full amenities. I had little privacy in this setting. At the time, I didn't value my worth or use my voice to express my concerns. I had much to learn.

My friend, Dee, also became a transition coordinator. We continued to be friends through good times and bad. The transition program at the university helped young adults with disabilities find further education or a job after high school. The program also provided help with independent living skills. I wanted to help people with disabilities build natural supports in the community.

I was about to experience transition planning in a unique setting! I took a graduate course on transition, but I did not have a deep understanding of transition planning and implementation of services. The doctoral class was tough, and my low self-esteem and fear of writing hindered me throughout the program. I was living an unbalanced existence, and I was nervous all the time about my performance at work and in classes. My work and achievement defined my identity. I believed that I had to do exceptionally well to gain acceptance as a qualified person.

The co-director told me about a client named Nola, a young lady who had gross motor skill impairments. She started the transition program at the same time I began the coordinator job. Dee and I went to meet her and began to build a relationship with the family. I had no idea then that I had just met a friend and a family I'd love for life. Nola restlessly walked around the room because of her motor skills deficiency; otherwise, she was a breath of fresh air! She was a cheerful woman who loved to joke around. She was playful and full of life. Her loving family—comprised of sister, mother, Grammy, and Pop-pop—supported her enthusiastically. Dolly and I were there to oversee transition and education services as part of a contract between the local school district and her family.

Between Dee and I, people quickly identified the friend and the supervisor, or how to maintain work boundaries. This inequality caused rifts between us at times. We were both still healing from our own childhood trauma. I became consumed with work, which increased my depression, anxiety, stress, and weight gain. I did not intend this to happen, but the pain of my past had not just magically disappeared. I tried to cover my feelings of inadequacy by proving that I could be the best in the doctoral program. I was always encouraging others but did little to nurture myself.

Later that year, I took a graduate course to learn how to write up a proposal for my first intervention study. My advisor met with me to identify a topic, but she did not read the entire proposal. This oversight led to many errors and resulted in my having to answer some hard questions and rewrite sections of the paper. My fear of failure and low self-confidence in writing skills were at their peak. I felt stuck in a terrible place as I continually replayed the failures over and over in my head. My emotional, physical, and spiritual state rested on shaky ground.

I continued to pour all of my energy into my doctoral work and my role as a transition coordinator. I worked with families to empower students to find their voice. Students with disabilities soon were creating PowerPoint presentations to highlight their goals, dreams, and future aspirations. Nola was part of the meeting and was able to talk about herself without running around the room. This occasion was the first time she felt empowered to speak about her life goals. Her mom and grandparents began to cry in joyous disbelief that Nola was leading the meeting. She was able to sit at the table for at least 30 minutes before leaving the room. Her family would remember this poignant moment for a long time. Everyone in our program began making these presentations in their selfled meetings.

Falafel Was the Common Factor

I was 30 years old as a second-year doctoral student. My intervention study was finally ready to be implemented by the end of the year. Due to my work and schoolwork, I had little time to date anyone. I met Jewelz in the summer while I was working at a local bar and restaurant. He was the chef, and I would often bring food from the kitchen to the tables. He was not very nice to me during my brief time working at the bar. But a few months later, Jewelz saw me when I was out with friends at another bar called the Firehouse. I was wearing a black dress with gold shoes. He asked for my number, and the rest is history. Our relationship was stressful. He didn't have a car, and he was not ambitious about his life goals. I did not see the blatant red warning flag, not at all, but I should have known. To clarify, I understand that the lack of a car doesn't mean a man is a player or a loser. Plenty of men who own cars are players. They're not ready for relationships and don't have the emotional maturity to maintain them. However, he exhibited symptoms that he was not in a healthy place mentally or emotionally, and I ignored those signs. For example, instead of waiting for him to get enough money to take me out to dinner, I chose to go to his house the first time we were together. I must emphasize the lack of wisdom in this decision. I made a poor choice and ended up spending the night with him. He would often smoke pot in the evening and was always watching television. The poor state of our relationship was a match for my current state of mind. I was not fully alive or present, and I did not know my worth. He would occasionally mistreat me, and I took the few crumbs of 'love' he sent my way. I freely allowed this man to keep me as a secondary priority in his life. In short, this man did not know how to love me well because he did not know God, who is the source of deep true love.

Jewelz certainly had abusive tendencies. When he yelled at me, I was afraid he would hit me. He was obsessed with calling me at times. If I said anything about his mistreatment of me and warned of a possible break-up, he would threaten to hurt himself. The only thing we had in common was falafel. No kidding. I always paid for his, and he never paid for mine. I was in such a state of self-loathing that I felt unworthy of love. I was finally able to break up with him later that year, and I wouldn't answer his phone calls anymore.

I met George the next summer. There was an attraction brewing between us, and I was pleased because he was a Christian. We sometimes talked after class, but then I did not see him around the rest of the summer.

Months later, Jewelz (the chef) and I began to talk once again. He came over to my house, and we 'made up.' He left soon after the 'making-up' session and called me later. I did not express myself then, about how I felt so wretchedly cheap, like second best. I was so upset with myself that I had relinquished a piece of my soul once more.

I was still living with the two clients (the men with disabilities) in an unstable environment. I had no clue how complacent I had become, living in this unhealthy atmosphere. "The body truly does keep score."[1] I was struggling in all areas of my life: emotionally, physically, spiritually,

---

1. Bessel Van Der Kolk, 2014

and sexually. I had no idea how much this emotional pain was deeply affecting every physical system in my body. I felt immense pain in my body. The greatest pain was deep in my back. I had gained additional weight as my inner self continued to shrivel away into a lifeless shell.

I was miserable with Jewelz, and I knew he was not the one for me, but I stayed with him anyway. I was desperate for connection in this season of my life. I would cry and beg him to stay so that I would not feel the deep sting of abandonment once again. I desperately wanted to be with a man, even someone who dished out abuse, instead of facing my intense loneliness. My wounds of abandonment and rejection were festering, and I had no desire to look in the mirror.

In the spring semester, I ran into George again in the education building, and he took me out for coffee and a movie. When we returned to the house, he gave me a brief kiss on the cheek. Later that evening, I went to Jewlz's house and spent the night, but this time without any physical intimacy. The next day I broke up with him for good.

George and I talked a lot; our interest in each other was mutual. But once again, my habit of ignoring blatant warning signs was still active. He told me about how he had been dating someone who then began to stalk him. I was unaware that George had issues. His pattern was to show excessive interest in a woman and then flee in fear when the commitment became too real. We talked about many things; he shared stories about his life in the navy, I spoke about my interests, and we discussed our shared passion for teaching and supporting youth. His goal was to wait until marriage to have sex, and I approved and respected his views. This desire was at the core of my heart; however, I was having trouble with the follow-through.

My second date with George was so romantic. He took me on a tour of several different wineries. After the second winery, he put his arms around me. By the third one, we had our first romantic kiss on a hilly vineyard path surrounded by rustic scenery. We enjoyed our leisurely ramble to the last winery of the day. We not only enjoyed each other's company— we were captivated. This word is the key. We didn't really know each other, and today I would not label our emotions as love; it was infatuation. The excitement of a new relationship can obscure perceptions; getting to know someone takes time.

George met my family a few weeks later, and then he took me to introduce me to his family. We were to go hiking with his brother and sister-in-law. His conservative Christian family attended a local church in town. I wore a dress instead of pants to dinner. Usually, I love wearing jeans and pants. However, I was hiding my insecurities behind dresses and skirts, attempting to hide my weight gain. I stayed overnight in the spare bedroom at his parents' house. On the way back home, he told me he was disappointed that I did not dress like his family because they wore jeans. In retrospect, I wondered, why should I have to do that? I unknowingly hid the best parts of myself because I did not recognize my true identity. Now I am comfortable with my own personality and style. I can be myself and accept love from the people who will walk by my side.

I spent many nights with George on many occasions, and we tested sexual boundaries. One weekend, he took me to visit with family friends and their children. I wore a dress then, and I thought we had an enjoyable time. But on the way home, he began to change his manner of speech and became argumentative towards me. I knew something was different. I was learning to exercise my gift of discernment and felt anxious. I did not hear from him for the rest of the weekend. My rejection issues and fear of abandonment rapidly surfaced.

A few days later, he wanted to meet me at the coffee shop where we had our first date. This event happened a scant three weeks after we began dating. I drove to the coffee shop that Monday afternoon. Before I went into the shop, I sat in my car, sending a loud cry out to God telling Him I could only go into that coffee shop if I had peace. I waited, motionless in my car, and didn't move until the peace of God came upon me entirely. I thanked God; then, I went inside the shop. I saw George come inside the store looking like a train hit him. His countenance revealed stress and anxiety. We got our coffee and then went upstairs to the second floor.

He was so nervous he spilled his coffee on the table. I began laughing nervously, not spitefully, but because I could not help it. He never got that upset, and I am usually the one to spill my coffee on myself, the table, or all over the place. I often laugh to try to break the tension and to help the other person feel more comfortable and laugh, too. But he did not laugh. He was beyond stressed. We found paper towels and began to clean up the table; the spill was no big deal. He started telling me about a dream he had about me and spiders that confirmed he should break up with me. I was not so much into a prophetic interpretation of dreams, then, but today, my reflection and understandings are different. I listened to him go on about the breakup and how he needed space. I calmly listened as he kept talking. I continued to sip my coffee, still sensing the peace of God within me. He went on and on about the rationale for this breakup until I interrupted him mid-sentence. I told him that I had to leave. I knew it was time to go before my supply of peace would dwindle.

I got up quietly and said goodbye to him. I walked down the stairs, out the door, and briskly got in my car. As soon as I shut the door, I began to weep. I was hurting so bad, full of sadness, and in deep pain. The weeping turned to wailing until I was barely able to breathe or speak. I did care about him! Or was I feeling triggered by former scenarios of rejection and abandonment? After a few minutes, I finally caught my breath, and as I drove across town, I called my friend Jen. I could barely manage to explain what was going on. I was a mess. I called Molly next, and I could barely speak between sobs. She listened to me and helped me calm down. I had no idea I was suffering from a panic attack triggered by the abandonment, rejection, and deep wounds.

Once again, another man had left my life. I did not want to believe it at the time, but this man was not for me. He seemed to have all the desirable characteristics of the man I would marry. He was a Christian, but he wanted to buy a house and live the regular Christian lifestyle of complacency. I was not in an emotionally healthy state, but I knew my life would be vastly different in the future. I started thinking about another guy I had dated a few times during my master's degree, who also wanted a house and a typical Christian lifestyle. But at that point, I realized that reviewing the list of all the people who had dealt me a hand of rejection wasn't helping my current state of mind.

I talked with God as I processed the breakup of this short-lived relationship with George. God brought me back to a lesson that He wanted to help me learn: *God is my only constant. He is the only source of consistency and security in my life. He knows me, loves me, and wants me to spend time with Him often. God is pleased with me despite my imperfections.* God is perfect, and He knew I would make mistakes. I am His creation, made alive by His breath, thought, and spoken word. I continued processing my intense, painful feelings with God the best I knew how.

George hoped to obtain a job at Lehigh through one of the community-based programs. I did not sit in on his interview for the residential program out of respect. When I saw him, I presented a warm and kind front and smiled impersonally, while all of my insides were so raw from the pain. I was learning how to keep my emotions together, but some days, I still fell apart despite my brave efforts. One afternoon, I darkened the office so I could weep. Afterward, one of my friends mentioned my weight gain, which was a very sensitive subject. Her brash approach sent a dagger even further into my heart. My struggle with body image and lack of self-love was an area of deep pain. I despised what was happening to me, but I had no idea how to help myself get better.

A month later, following the breakup with George, I got a call from my ex-boyfriend Jewelz. I was at such a place of low self-esteem, poor self-worth, and general loathing that my inward turmoil and outward appearance revealed deep pain and emptiness. I did not value myself at all. I was emotionally exhausted with the topic of friendships with men. My heart was in shreds once again. My anxiety increased also, and I tried to distract myself by working overtime and on schoolwork.

A Change of Focus

I began writing the results of my completed research intervention study. My new advisor preferred to have a second advisor continue to co-lead the process. My presentation of the study and results went well, but several revisions of the paper were needed to move forward in the process. This rewrite was even more stressful, but I was determined to move on. I became very assertive in my independent design and implementation of the entire study. I did not know this process was building me up for later life lessons.

During the latter half of 2010, I became interested in volunteering at church. I met with one of the pastors, Ale, who supported my involvement with children's ministry. I felt joyful as I worked once a month with preschool children, helping them with crafts and snacks. This time brought back memories as a teenager, helping my mom with the children at my first church.

I continued to take doctorate courses and stayed on as a transition coordinator. This year, we instituted a new calendar design to alternate weeks so that transition coaches could work with a variety of individuals to avoid burnout. We also built connections with families. I enjoyed hanging out with all of the clients. They flourished with connection, empowerment, and support to help them find their hidden voice. I loved to see this in action.

Oh, There You Are

In 2011, we hired new people to work at several of the university community-based programs. The early interviews were intended to support graduate students with a stipend and paid tuition. A man named Bud was one of the applicants. I was not a part of his interview process, but I heard exceptional reports about him. One semester later, I noticed him walking down the hall past my office. He was a very handsome Black Latino man with a muscular build. I stuck my head out the door as he passed down the hallway, and we exchanged a glance and a hello. As he walked by, my first thought was, Oh, there you are. This thought went to the back of my mind, and I didn't think about it until a few years later. I occasionally crossed paths with him during training sessions. He was in the counseling psychology degree program, and I had done my best to avoid that field. I felt inadequate and unqualified to work in that field due to my past. In late winter of 2011, I met Bud by chance at a grocery store on a Friday evening. I was surprised he would be shopping there, but I'm not sure why, because everyone goes to the grocery store to buy food. I spoke cheerfully to him, and he nodded to me in a friendly manner on his way out the door.

A Gradual Shift Back Towards God

I had attended Life Church since returning to PA in 2006, but I was not involved in church activities. I hoped to remain unnoticed by sitting in the middle section, and I only spoke to a few people in that area. The youth director gave the message in one service; his talk was delightful, but I wasn't ready for active involvement yet. I was comfortably invisible. I began to get involved with children's ministry in 2010. Later the following year, in March, I was eager to work with the young adults, so I applied to Life Church. That next month, I interviewed with April, who had just returned from a mission trip to Haiti. After that, I began attending youth nights as an observer. I was amazed to see hundreds of youth gathered in the auditorium of the church. The first night I was there, many of the students were emotionally distraught about losing their home due to a fire. I was in tears as I sympathetically listened to them, and knew I was in the right place. After a few months, I began a small women's Bible study and met with some of the youth group girls weekly before the large meeting started. We used Francis Chan's book, Crazy Love. Hannah, Madicyn, Yadeliz, and a few other girls were part of this study. After a few weeks, we began meeting at a different, quieter location. I enjoyed my time with the girls and always brought pizza. I held back, though, and did not let my personality burst out. I have continued to remain in contact with some of them, especially Yadeliz, with whom I have a deep connection. She is my friend, sister, and prayer-warrior partner for life.

I met the youth pastor, Devon, his wife, Yalli, and the entire team. We were continually evolving as a leadership group. Another woman on the team was also working on her doctoral degree. I told her I had often been eager to join the youth group team in the past, but it was not suitable with my schedule.

My first year as a youth leader was tumultuous, owing to my emotional, spiritual, and physical states. Every time I attended a Wednesday night service, it was as if a light illuminated my entire being. The instant I left that atmosphere, however, I felt as if my light dimmed. I still felt unlovable and very self-conscious about my weight gain. I was painfully self-aware, yet so clueless about how to find solutions to my problems.

The Transition to a New Advisor

I didn't have as many classes to attend then because the doctoral program requirements were changing. I worked with students and edited my papers. My new co-advisor was hard to figure out. I was getting to know her more by co-teaching a class with her than by socializing that semester. I often filled in for her when she was unable to teach due to her health flareups. At first, I was nervous about co-teaching with her after hearing that another doctoral student who worked with her left her office crying. The doctoral student was a friend who lost her brother from suicide the year before; she went home for the funeral, but when she returned, she was not the same. We were close friends for a few years, and I grieved to see that she did not seem to recover. I had cared so much for my friend. That was another lesson: sometimes, *people in pain respond differently than expected. Then again, expectations of how someone else will handle grief can easily lead to judgment.* I can attest to this. When I was emotionally raw, I did not respond from a place of mental stability. People with deep wounds and severe pain often hurt others' feelings. But those who pursue ongoing healing can be part of other people's restoration.

In November 2011, I had a case of bronchitis that worsened with each day. The following story is something I did not make up, embarrassingly enough. I had read about a farmer who survived the bubonic plague by putting an onion pierced with a fork in a corner of the barn. The onion was able to absorb the plague, and the man later attributed his escape from death to his natural remedy. I read this story while I was sick, so I thought it would be a great idea to try. I purchased a red onion, put a fork in it, and slept next to it overnight. However, I became sicker, and I barely had anything to eat or drink. Obviously, the sickness I had was not the plague.

On the third day, my mom ran an errand to buy me soup. That evening, it took me almost an hour to get out of bed and go downstairs. When my mom arrived, I told her not to come inside but to follow me to the emergency room. At the ER, the nurse immediately took me back for an examination. I had a fever near 105. Doctors were wondering if I needed to get a spinal tap to assess for meningitis. This was extremely alarming for me, but the initial results showed that I had pneumonia. I was very weak. It felt as if I had a ton of bricks on my chest, and my breathing was labored. My oxygen level was at 89, whereas a normal oxygen level should be near 100. I was admitted to the hospital overnight. This was the first time I spent the night in the hospital since I was born. I had IVs, heart monitors, water, and oxygen pumping all at once. That evening, all I could hear was the continuous sound of the monitors. I felt so scared and alone.

In the hospital, I texted Jewelz, and he said it was too much trouble to walk and see me. My heart sank. I do not know why I stayed with this man. My state of mind falsely said I deserved all of this hardship. Sweat was dripping down my back as the fever began to break. My chest was weak and I was coughing continuously. The bronchitis-to-pneumonia switch was sudden; my immune system was at its worst ever. I felt deathly ill, like I was fighting for my life. The next day, doctors reviewed my vitals and took chest X-rays. Throughout the night, my oxygen level had dropped to 84, so I remained in the hospital another whole day.

On the second evening, my parents came to visit. I was usually the strong one, so it was difficult to be seen in my visibly weakened state with oxygen support. I felt helpless. I texted one of the other youth leaders and asked her to notify the other team members that I had pneumonia and that I was in need of prayer. They all prayed for me.

That night, whenever I closed my eyes, I saw these awful visions of thousands of people with grey skin, trying to harm each other. I could not close my eyes without seeing these images. I was frightened. At one point, I was so anxious that my blood pressure had risen to 185/100. I was having ongoing panic attacks, but I somehow managed to get to sleep later. I was talking with God but still felt so far away from Him. The next day, I had not moved at all, and my chest still felt as if someone were sitting on it. I was so weak. But an hour before I was scheduled to go home that afternoon, Devon came to visit me and pray with me. He was the only other person, besides my parents, that came to visit me. That small act of kindness meant so much to me then, and even to this day. God sends people with love and humility to you when you need it. Devon and his wife, Yalli, are dear to my heart.

The day I left the hospital, it took almost all my strength just to walk out the door into the bitter cold. I spent a whole week recuperating at my parents' home. I finally went back to work the following week while continuing to recover.

A month later, I heard that the youth were going to go on a missions trip to Haiti in June 2012. I knew this was the trip for me; I felt in my heart that I needed to go. I began to save money for Haiti. I had never been outside the country, besides Canada, and I needed a passport. I was learning more about God and desired to move closer to Him, yet I still kept Him at a distance. I was in a state of dark depression and often felt the heaviness of burdens that I was carrying for myself and others.

My ongoing backpain issues would often flare up during the week. Sometimes in the computer lab at Lehigh, I would fall to the floor in excruciating pain. Years later, I learned that sciatica might be due to lack of emotional support, abandonment, and the burden of financial stresses. The level of pain in my back increased in the months leading up to this trip. I was baptized at church in March. I felt very free as I was plunged into the water. God had so much more for my life, and this was the beginning!

The Gift of Teaching

In April, Devon and Yalli invited me to speak at youth group and gave me a topic to teach on. They had no idea about my teaching skills development over the years. I created a PowerPoint for the main presentation. During this lesson, God was purposeful in giving me a life-scripture that I would read, pray over, meditate on, and live out with Him. Joshua 1:8 (KJV) reads, "This book of the law shall not depart out of thy mouth; but thou shalt meditate therein day and night, that thou may observe to do according to all that is written therein: for then thou shalt make thy way prosperous, and then thou shalt have good success." This verse struck deep in my heart. Meditating on God's word day and night would lead me into the best path of my life. The next verse would help me move forward as well. Joshua 1:9 (KJV) says, "Have not I commanded thee? Be strong and of a good courage; be not afraid, neither be thou dismayed, for the Lord thy God is with thee withersoever thou goest." The lesson was on safety rails and boundaries. I found that subject to be particularly amusing because I love driving on roads without guardrails, since it feels more adventurous. The message was that guard rails are from God; He sent people who could love me by providing correction with wisdom at times of need. I was passionate about this lesson, and I adapted it to my youth group audience using additional materials I'd prepared for the evening. I prayed and asked God for help, and He alleviated my nerves before the session.

Yalli came over to see if I needed anything before teaching. I answered that I was okay, but I was thankful that she checked with me. After worship and prayer, it was time to speak. Well, as soon as I began, I captured the attention of the youth. My passion about the word of God and about teaching was visible. My gift of teaching was highlighted. Devon and Yalli agreed that it was one of my gifts and invited me to do more teaching. God knew when it was time for me to be revealed like an arrow with a sword of truth and love. I love how Devon and Yalli empowered me to use my voice. They may have been unsure about my ability, but they still gave me the freedom to try. My light began to shine because they encouraged me. *True leaders empower others and allow them to make mistakes.*

Keep the Dim Light Going

My teaching session was a bright light before more difficult days drew near. I continued to prepare for the Haiti trip. Aside from attending youth group, I felt almost absent from my body. It was as if parts of my personality weren't even there. By the end of April, I was in a severe depression, and at one of my darkest and lowest points. When I look back, it was as if I were reverting to my sixth-grade self, often sitting in the dark attic, feeling lonely and unworthy. I had only fleeting moments of hope. My concerned family sat me down for a talk before leaving for the Haiti trip. My mom asked me to share my feelings, and my sister said I seemed detached. I began sobbing, as I often did back then, when people began pointing out some obvious and not-so-obvious pain. I didn't know where all of my pain and sorrow was coming from; I couldn't remember parts of my younger years. Here I was, at 31, struggling to understand my life. I felt a sudden vulnerability, shame, guilt, embarrassment, sorrow and pain, but I had no idea of the root issues. As I was crying, I told my family that I felt closer to my long-term goal of being in Africa. I had several friends tell me that there was nothing holding me back from going, except for the commitment to my schooling. I was not truly free, but I hid behind my intellect and academics all those years. I told my family I was excited to go to Haiti and that I knew change was coming soon.

In May, I worked on finishing the final draft for my last qualifier study defense. I was so anxious to write perfectly and complete everything that I could not freely write. I would often feel blocked when I tried to write, due to a deep fear that nothing would come out with perfect accuracy and clarity. Following my presentation, I had more editing to do on the paper. My presentation was always my strong point. I knew how to prioritize and design the presentation well, but my papers were not so well-organized. My executive functioning skills were extremely weak at the time. I had not been able to gain much relief from past trauma and had not dealt with my current emotional, physical, spiritual, and sexual health concerns. The effects of past trauma were constantly influencing everything in my life, but I didn't understand any of this yet.

Once the committee accepted the study and results, I had three months to prepare for the comprehensive exams in September. I researched every topic and wrote down all of the essays so I could memorize the information for my answers on the big exam day.

Silent No Longer

Chapter 5

Why am I surrounded by my own condemnation?
Why did I allow unworthiness and harm to surround me?

The Adventure to Haiti

My trip to Haiti began on June 14th and ended June 23rd. The team was going to an orphanage that cared for 30 children. The flight was relatively short. The team was made up of people whom I still care about today and keep in contact with or think about often. We met early in the morning and prayed together before we boarded the van and drove to the airport.

Upon the arrival in Haiti, we knew to grab our luggage and keep moving through the airport without making eye contact or allowing people to help us because they would charge fees for the help. We got through quickly, although the eyes of many people were upon us. All twelve of us got in the van with Dario, our interpreter for the trip. The heat felt amazing, like Arizona weather. On the way to the orphanage, I soon noticed the extreme poverty and desperation of people around me. Babies were walking around naked, the roads were unpaved, and people were living in collapsing and decaying buildings. My heart began to stir with sorrow and grief. As we went through the town, I saw a hill covered with thousands of tents; people were still living there three years after the devastating earthquake that took many lives. The trip to the orphanage took approximately thirty minutes. The van drove through a set of tall doors down the pathway to the orphanage. The property contained a house, a church with a roof (but no walls), and a large dirt yard for the children to play sports. Many children ran up to the van to greet us. Some of the children took our luggage. I was amazed to see small children lifting luggage that was bigger than they were and carrying it to the house. The children followed us into the house to help.

The team members chose to put our tents on the top of the roof. I was in the tent with April and another woman. After setting up the tents, we climbed down the ladder to have lunch. Several women cooked and served lunch for us. The home had a bathroom, adjacent kitchen, a hallway, and a large family room. Immediately, we found out rather quickly that the toilet in the bathroom did not work well so we had to use a large bucket to help the toilet flush. Additionally, we had to use well water to bathe.

Lunch was a delicious spread of a red beets, chicken wings, beans, rice, and salad. We appreciated the women's effort. Following lunch, we spent time outside in the hot sun, meeting the children and playing games. The team began to bond that week. We enjoyed being with the pastor and children during Bible school. Every day we had devotions and worship in the morning and the evening. I will always remember a line from one song we sang, accompanied by guitar music, "From the rising of the sun, the name of the Lord is to be praised." We were encouraged to write our experiences in a journal. God began moving in my heart the first day. I did not fully understand my giftings back then, but I am extremely sensitive to the land. This means that I can sense the atmosphere of the spiritual realm around me.

That first evening, I fell asleep easily. I awoke to the din of barking dogs, bleating goats, and the even noisier roosters, accompanied by the sound of voodoo worship coming from the hills. The spiritual atmosphere became intense at times overnight due to the demonic spirit-worship. Prayer covering was important for all of us. Other mornings, we woke up to the beautiful sound of the children singing. They would gather at the side of the house waiting for us to awaken. My heart softened more and more as we spent time playing soccer, jumping ropes, and just loving the children.

In the evenings, I learned how to wear a headlight and how to brush my teeth with a bottle of water. Later on, I remember a young man from the team asking me about my testimony. While thinking, I realize I did not have a specific moment about the first time I believed in God. I had grown up in a Lutheran church thinking I always 'knew God.' I kept that thought.

During vacation Bible school time with the children, I talked about Paul's conversion with the support of a translator. The gospel message was being demonstrated according to the teaching of Jesus Christ. It rained one day; the children were afraid of rain because it reminded them of landslides, so they ran indoors. We did not have a huge rainstorm until later.

Pastor Guitone came over to me before it began to rain because he saw I was having difficulty getting my feet clean. He bent down and began pouring water over my dirty feet. I thanked him but felt that I was there to help and serve him and the children instead. His health was poor that week, and here he was serving me. I wept later at the loving act he did for me by the well. He had a heart like that of Papa God. The Father was drawing me in and metaphorically cleansing my feet. I realize now that this was part of my becoming a disciple of the Lord. I felt so honored to receive the gift of His love! It was challenging for me to receive Papa God's love, but in time, my hard heart slowly became pliable.

One of the main purposes for the team's trip to the orphanage was to build playground equipment for the children. Construction began the following morning when additional pastors from the church arrived with materials. The senior pastor at my church, Pastor Randy, helped build it with some other men. While most of the men worked on building the playground, many of the women on the team spent time with the children. It was incredible to see everyone working together with the Haitians to build the children a new playground!

The next day, one of the women making lunch was accidentally burned by hot oil. Pastor Randy and one of the other pastors took her to the hospital for treatment. I felt so sad for one of her little children, who was screaming and crying. No one was able to calm her. Just then, I saw another little girl bringing the crying girl towards me. I thought in my head, *God, please do not bring her to me. I will cry and I do not want to cry in front of the children. It will make it worse for them.* I remember Him saying, "You can cry." As soon as I held her on my lap with my arms around her, she was quiet and calm. I began crying. Five of the young girls gathered around us in a circle; they gave her a bottle. Instantly, I began to think that I should help with this but the girls were doing a good job. That beautiful moment taught me that we nurture one another with love during and after our stay in the womb and on earth. This day wrecked my heart for the girls. I kept crying as I held some of the older girls and could sense their deep pain of abuse and trauma.

Later that day, the rain began to pour down. All the kids fled to their rooms in fear. The leaders started bringing our bags down to the main floor where April and I were catching suitcases. At one point, we began to laugh and dance in the rain together. I felt like God was restoring some lost childhood freedom and laughter in that moment. April and I both experienced a connection with each other, and we were just so joyful! That point was definitely the beginning of a strong friendship. April later became a dear sister whom I consider a confidant and lifelong friend. We continue to see that God is leading our friendship. I am thankful for her; she has been through similar traumatic situations as I have, and our family history is similar in several ways.

The team kept the suitcases downstairs from then on to keep them safe from any future rain. That week, God continued to remind me that intimacy with Him was so much more important than perfection and performance.

I was having intense reactions to the land. I had no clue about the spiritual warfare that we would encounter. One night, it became extremely cold on the roof, lower than normal temperatures. Four of us who had sexual abuse trauma had nightmares that evening. I made that connection from the night before. I was really battling with my thoughts and the renewal of my mind. My back was in pain most of the week. I had difficulty expressing how I was feeling. God led me to Exodus 14:14, which reads, "I, the Lord your God, will fight for you; you only need to be still." I felt like I had been through many battles but had no idea what it all meant. The Lord also began to highlight Joshua 1:9, telling me not to be afraid and to be of good courage. Over the course of the trip, God led me to Deuteronomy 30 to let me know that

He would fight for me and that I was not to look to the left or right, but to Him. I was struggling mentally that week, but did not talk about it due to embarrassment and the fear of judgment.

Near the end of the trip, we spent time relaxing at a local beach and visited some cultural areas of the city. I learned something about Haiti's history. On the way back, I felt depressed by the wretched display of poverty and the realization that people were still recovering from the earthquake devastation. We returned to the orphanage, but that night was a difficult night. Most of us felt sick from the effects of eating foreign food, even though we had gone to a nice restaurant. I was definitely not feeling well.

The women in the kitchen kindly gave us oatmeal that evening for dinner. Later on, the last night of the trip, I talked with April and Lindsay on the rooftop. I had been chosen to do the closing devotional that evening. I was in pain from my back, so they began to pray for healing. I felt my back improving and I ran around the rooftop full of joy! I rushed downstairs to share the news with everyone. But when I burst excitedly into the room, I sensed that the mood was very somber. The team was sad because we would be departing for home in the morning. We sat with the children and held many of them in our arms. After they left for the evening, I began talking about 1 Corinthians 13 and how love is the huge center of everything. If we do not have love, we are a clanging symbol. We were learning how to love others well during this trip, and in the process, our own hearts were knit together. We finished packing before breakfast the next morning. Afterward, we went downstairs to meet as a group.

A Change of Heart

As we gathered in a circle, Guitone was on my left and Devon was on my right. We began to pray for the children and for Guitone and his family. Devon sensed that there was someone in the room who had been water baptized but still needed to recognize Jesus Christ as Lord. The first time he said it, no one moved. He said it again, and instantly I fell to my knees weeping. I received words of affirmation pouring over me from the team and Papa God. I heard phrases such as, "You are the apple of His eye" and "God loves you, and you are His daughter." Everyone laid hands on me as I sobbed for what felt like an eternity. When I finally got up, I sensed newfound joy, peace, and love! I had known Jesus as Savior, but now Jesus was my Lord! This was the beginning of my deeper surrender and journey with the Lord. I was full of joy all that day and on the flight home. As the vans brought us back from the airport to the church, my brother and mother were there waiting for me. My brother asked me if we had had any encounter with voodoo because he was in my old bedroom at my parent's house and his phone kept ringing at 3 a.m. While I was in Haiti, at 3 a.m. in Allentown, my dad began laughing maniacally, so much so that my mom left the bedroom they shared upstairs. *The thought is daunting when we realize how the spiritual atmosphere in one place can influence another place at the same time.*

This is often part of generational strongholds. These patterns continue to influence future descendants if the root issues are not addressed. I was freer than I was before this trip to Haiti, but now I knew that spiritual warfare is a reality. My brother also felt spiritually attacked at home. I had been praying for him on several occasions and continued to keep him in prayer. The warfare was intense. But I was so full of joy my family did not know what to do with me! This trip brought me more freedom and more intimacy with the Lord!

The next week, the Haiti team shared stories about our trip with the entire youth group! I was now out of my shell and was coming into the reality of my true self! However, a few weeks after my return, I suddenly felt more fear, began weeping every night, and kept my lights on all night for almost two months in a row! I wept as God took me through Psalm 78, the chapter about the rebellious years of Israel. They had been close to God, but then they drifted far from him. God was showing me this was how I had behaved and that I still did not trust Him. I was full of sorrow and wept at the revelation. I also began to realize that He speaks with me through the Bible, through prophetic words, and through other people. I knew that God was near me because He is close to the broken-hearted (Psalm 34:18).

Completing the Comprehensive Exams

In September 2012, Dee and I both took the first part of the comprehensive exams of the doctoral degree process and found out that we passed a month later. I was one step closer to my Ph.D.! The second part of the exam involved an-alyzing two different types of study-design articles. I spent a lot of time crying as I wrote the group design critique. A few weeks later, I heard that I did extremely well on the group design article but not as well on the single subject design. On the group design article, I highlighted the verbs in each sentence to help me write succinctly, which was challenging for me at the time. As a result, I had to defend the critique I wrote in an oral exam because of the inaccurate summary of the single subject research critique. I was so anxious over this process. My core beliefs were "I am not worthy, loved, or valued," and this led me to sink down deeper into this false belief. I read and re-read the single-subject design paper. On the day of the defense, I was nervous. Earlier in the week, I spoke with the research director to see if I could get a substi-tute at work so that I would have preparation time on the day of the oral defense. This request was denied. I had to cover for a classroom and then come back to Lehigh to defend my paper. Prior to the defense, I began praying to God for peace of mind, but at the forefront of my thoughts was the deep fear of failure. As soon as I began my presentation at the de-fense, I felt as if I could not speak clearly. My tongue was not working normally and I felt frozen. I could not explain the strengths or weaknesses of the design, so I tried to demon-strate my knowledge on the board. After about forty-five minutes or so, Dr. Kern said they would follow up with me at a later time. I left the building with such heaviness and sadness. I wept when I got to my car. Later, I reached out to my friend Robin. Fortunately, I was watching Robin's chil-dren that night, which would keep my mind from thinking about this epic failure. Dolly and Kyle also came over for support. I was even crying while watching a movie with the kids. We did have boatloads of fun to keep my mind in the present, but it was challenging. On the way home that night, it was pouring rain, which seemed appropriate to my frame of mind. As I drove up a hill towards the apartment, my crying became more intense. I was crying so hard that I had to pull over to the side of the road. As I wept, I looked up and followed the direction of the car lights pointing directly to a car parked in front of me. The word "Jesus" shone brightly from a silver plaque on the car ahead. I took a deep breath and in that moment knew Jesus was saying I was going to get through this time.

Finish What You Start

I went up to my room, wept all night, and barely got myself up the next morning. I was at the gym when God reminded me to go finish what I had started. I had heard that same statement prior to the oral exam defense. The next morning, I went to church, although I was full of depression, shame, and despair. Another reminder from God came in the form of Pastor Randy saying, at least twice during the service, to finish what you start. I knew God was speaking directly to me.

Later, Dr. Kern sent me an email saying that the faculty had never seen me struggle to speak or express myself before. So they offered a remedy for the situation; I was to enroll in a single subject design course the next semester, and after passing this course, I would have to write a second single-design article critique for the faculty to review. I had to qualify and receive a loan quickly in order to make the deadline for this course, an online class offered by a school in Chicago. I sent the loan submission on Monday, and by Wednesday the deposit was complete! God had a huge surprise for me with this uncommon turnaround. It usually takes three weeks for the 403b loan to process, but it was complete in less than three days! God is faithful! He was showing me His plans to help me finish what I start!

Tumbling Through the Turbulence

I was headed into another tumultuous season of my life as I began my fourth year of the doctoral program. This year, I wrote up the final results of my qualifier study on vocabulary and I was learning how to design studies. I also made plans to defend my dissertation proposal.

At the end of 2011, I decided to leave my role as a transition coordinator to intern with my current advisor, a part-time position funded by a reading grant. My research subject was vocabulary for secondary students with Reading Disabilities. The transition to part-time would allow me more writing time.

I did not begin the new internship position until August 2012. There was a lot to do. Before I left my current position, I organized all of the folders on USBs to provide for the new coordinator. As I was familiar with the program, policies, and procedures, I knew how important it was to take the time to continue these connections and train the new coordinators as well.

Encounter on the Mountain

In December, our youth leadership team went to the Poconos for a retreat. I was working overnights at a community-based home in a part-time position and could not be there for the first session on Friday evening. As soon as my shift ended, I drove to meet the team for the remainder of the retreat.

When I arrived, everyone said that the Holy Spirit had fallen so powerfully the night before. I was excited about that, because I hungered and thirsted for a touch from God. I talked to different youth leaders that morning, and after breakfast, we all gathered in the living room for worship. Holy Spirit began to wreck our hearts as one of the youth played piano and led us in worship. I began to weep, and I could sense so many colors around me. All of a sudden, I felt as if someone put their hand inside of my back and squeezed my heart, as if to crumble my heart of stone. I did not realize my heart was stony at the time, but looking back, I realize it was! I could feel Holy Spirit begin His work. My heart began to flutter and beat very rapidly. I saw a blurry vision of something, most likely an angel, in front of me. I fell to the ground weeping, feeling intense love. But then, I began to overthink it. I looked around, thinking that maybe I was having a heart attack at the retreat. As I grew afraid, the moment came to a halt. I had a vision of Jesus' disciple Peter getting out of the boat, walking on water, and then falling into the water. Well, I could relate to Peter in that moment. The teaching at the retreat was about the conditions of the heart. We were asked to reflect on the healthy and unhealthy conditions of our heart. I asked God to show me my heart conditions, both the good and bad. April later spoke about the conditions of the heart and how that related to preparation as a soldier for the Lord. I again felt the power of the Holy Spirit. All of us were like minded with unity in the Lord during this retreat.

Devon spoke about a book an angel placed on his desk one morning, called Bless Your Spirit by Arthur Burk. We each had a copy, and I still read the book daily. I will never forget this natural and supernatural move of God and the encounter I had that weekend. It was yet another way God softened my heart toward Him.

The Move to Finish What I Began

During this cold winter, I began an online course to complete my comprehensive exam. In this single subject design course, we had online assignments with a required weekly, hour-long chat. The chat began with irrelevant discussion of the weather and other topics for approximately 25 minutes of the hour-long online discussion. This part of the class was annoying and felt like a waste of time. Fortunately, I acquired deep knowledge of designing research studies because of this course. At the end of the semester, I passed this course and did well on my single subject design article critique!

The next hurdle toward my doctorate was the dissertation proposal. I began writing chapters with my current advisor and I was in the process of getting approval from my co-advisor. Unfortunately, in the mix of all of this, my ex-boyfriend, Jewelz, had somehow snuck back into my life. Let me clarify; I chose to enter a relationship with a man who did not add value to my life. This was a clear indication as to my beliefs about my own lack of worth, value, and understanding as a woman. At the time, I had no idea about the origin of the roots of these unhealthy belief patterns.

Jewelz and I began talking again, and I invited him to my new apartment. I enjoyed having my own space and living in a new area of Bethlehem. I was no longer living with other people, and it was a necessary transition. Fortunately, we did not do anything but talk. He got a tour of the apartment and lounged on the couch. I laid my head on his chest as we talked. The conversation wasn't anything groundbreaking. In the next few weeks, I mostly talked with Jewelz on the phone. Fortunately (I thank God for this), Jewelz told me one day that he had found a new girlfriend. I cried listening to him tell me about her, but I was ultimately glad to remove myself from this situation. A few months later, I saw him at a grocery store with his new girlfriend and her children.

Shortly after, Jewelz contacted me and shared his girlfriend cheated on him. He asked me to hang out again and I said no. This was such protection from God! It took me a few years to understand soul ties and to release any bond Jewelz and I had through prayer and the blood of Jesus Christ. In this process, I was still recovering from feelings of self-hatred and lack of self-worth.

Love of My Life

While at work in November, I ran into Bud at the university. Bud was now a graduate student obtaining a degree in counseling psychology and working full time through a different program. Somehow, we began talking about life. Bud told me he was thinking about applying for the counseling psychology doctoral program following the completion of his master's degree in May 2014. I thought it was a wonderful idea and encouraged him to apply! He was nervous about the application process and taking the GRE exam. I shared my own GRE exam story and assured him that I got accepted into the doctoral program despite having a lower GRE score. The faculty knew my work ethic and performance in the master's program. After talking for a while, we exchanged phone numbers so we could meet up and review his doctoral student application essays. During our conversation, we'd also talked about our faith. A few hours after meeting with Bud, I searched for encouraging Scriptures for him and texted him a list of verses. He wrote back to thank me, and that some of them were Scriptures he'd read often.

We met up a few weeks later in my office. As I reviewed his application, it was disheartening to read what he had written. His essay discussed traumatic events and experiences he experienced as a child. I paused and looked up, my eyes meeting his gaze with compassion, but he flashed me a grin. I did not know him that well yet, but I learned that he often tried to mask his inner pain with a smile. I felt such empathy for him and his journey. I understood what that was like to a degree. In that moment, my entire being felt a nudge to give him a huge hug, but I held back. I was so grieved to know about those experiences he had in childhood. Because Bud was applying to a different program, I was unsure of this program's expectation for the essay, such as how much of his personal story he should include. He was also planning to meet with a different colleague for advice, and I thought that made sense. Over the next month, we texted back and forth.

Once we reconnected, Bud and I had ongoing conversations. One night, we made an impromptu decision to attend one of the night-watch services at a local Baptist church for New Year's Eve. Bud had grown up in a Baptist church. I had been to a night-watch service before and so had he. I remember what he wore to the night-watch service to this day. He had on a green button-down shirt, jeans, and brown dress shoes. He found a parking spot around 9:30 p.m. so that we had time to get good seats. After we entered the church building, he looked my way and smiled before leading the way up the stairs to the top floor. We sat on the left side of the building near the end of the row, much to my contentment. The service was beautiful. At one point, I sat on the floor just reveling in the Lord. I think I took him by surprise but it did not faze me. I waved at a little baby near where we sat most of the night. The night watch began with dance worship and flag waving in the front of the room. I was so glad to attend the night worship with Bud.

I cannot explain it, but being with Bud left me full of joy, peace, hope, and refreshment. I remember it like yesterday. I had pure enjoyment spending time with this man, and I did not have a clue as to why.

The New Year

The New Year brought deeper friendship with Bud as he continued in the application process. I would often text him random, silly stuff. I told him that I would treat him to Olive Garden to celebrate his application and admittance into the doctoral program. We discussed various topics over dinner, and somehow stumbled upon his interest in watching court cases as he described a particular case in detail. We ended up talking about people struggling with their sexuality.

At the end of the evening, we both left the restaurant laughing. Bud walked me to my car, where he gave me a hug. I loved his hugs. Later that week, we met at the gym a few times over a period of weeks. I was usually working out upstairs while he was downstairs doing his own routine. Bud has upper-body strength that I would love to have one day. The gym has two floors so I could see him down below doing twenty pull-ups, and he always made it look easy. I felt inspired by watching him because in my mind, it is a winning day if I could pull myself half-way up the pull-up support machine.

Revelation of a Man's Heart

In late February, God began showing me revelations about Bud. He is the only man God gave me revelation about, specifically concerning matters of the heart and the struggles he battled. Once, I had a disturbing vision of him with black flies coming out of his mouth. As I began mentally processing the meaning of the dream, I began to understand what God was showing me about his struggles with sexuality. I wept. I chose not to tell him about this. I was seeking God for counsel. Bud found out in March that he was accepted into the Ph.D. program. I knew this was a thrilling moment for him and I was so proud of him! He showed symptoms of PTSD, which sometimes leaked out during conversations when he was trying to determine my loyalty towards him. For example, one day as we were driving, he began talking about someone I knew, gauging how I would react if she told me something in private. I think he was wondering if he could be vulnerable and honest with me about his struggles.

An Upgraded Position

In spring of 2014, I was busy finalizing my dissertation edits and completing my study. One of the former doctoral students at Lehigh reached out to me about a position she had just left at a local intermediate unit to move to a higher level. I interviewed and got the job. The interviewers chose to hire me even after I forgot my USB in the car before my presentation. I knew it was God's promotion, independent from man's approval. They chose to wait for me to begin until after the study was complete in the summer. I was so grateful. Bud was happy for me, too. We were both transitioning into new roles in different places. We had become great friends by the end of that year. I went to his graduation at the university stadium and took some free gifts that were given to the families and friends entering the stadium to watch. Afterward, I ended up giving Bud this gift. Though he tried manipulating me into that decision, I knew what he was doing and gave it to him anyway. However, as we became closer, I would call him on it and tell him that I loved him and did not need to be convinced to help him with any form of manipulation. He just had to tell me the truth. I am thankful to be able to continue a relationship and show love to someone, yet state the truth and handle the relationship with care the best I knew how at the time.

Confirmation of the Revelation

Following graduation, Bud and I would text and talk, and he even helped me with my dissertation data. Early in

June, he was coming up to Lehigh to meet with me about the data sheets. I remember us having a funny conversation. I always laughed because as we got to know each other he would let me know about how far away he was or when he would get there. Bud and I had the type of relationship that we could tell what was going on with each other by a look in the eye. I could hear what he was not saying and vice versa. Our connection was at the eye, heart, and soul level, and really, the spirit level. It was a connection built by the Lord. It is the only way to explain that level of knowing so much about a person without many words.

I realize now that much of my time with him was spent trying to make him love me for who I was. I believe he did love me in the best way he knew how at the time. I did not understand and was striving at times for love for no reason. I often talk too much when I am anxious or to protect myself from my feelings that are all too real. Over time, I have learned how not to do that anymore, but it took a lot of healing.

A Different Revelation

In June of 2014, Bud said he was going to share something with me. I was typing away on the computer as he revealed to me that he was gay. I already knew what he was struggling with but to hear him speak it aloud was different. He didn't look at me when he was talking, unsure how I might take it. I could tell he felt shame, heaviness, and unworthiness, and my heart felt so sad. I told him to come near me and we were face to face, eye-to-eye, and heart to heart. I took him by the hands, as we often did when praying, and I told him he was a man of God. In that instance, he had to stop me and said it felt good to hear he was a man of God. I saw him soften to receive my love in prayers. I began praying over him, telling him that God had such good plans for his life. I said I would love him no matter what because he was my friend. He smiled in relief. He thought he would lose my friendship. As he left. he sent a gaze back to me with a wide grin that I was staying in his life. I did love him and I would stay. You see, at the time, I loved Bud and our connection, but it still was at a deep friendship level. After he was gone, I closed my door and wept. I did not grow up learning how to express emotions and feelings in front of other people all of my life. I had to be the 'strong one.' Today, I would have wept in front of Bud. I would not hold back on expressing my true feelings. Perhaps, we could have wept together. I do not know. Later, I went home and wept most of the evening. I made salsa and invited him to come over to sit on my front porch steps to talk and enjoy the warm summer weather.

My new job started in August. Since Bud was going to school too, we would often meet to do schoolwork together. I would sometimes give him advice or just provide support in general. When I spoke of my past abuse, I was touched to hear him speak of me in a protective role as a man.

Bud's Injury

Near the end of August, Bud and I had plans to get together on a Friday evening. When Friday evening arrived, I didn't hear from him. He never cancelled plans before without letting me know. I texted him but did not get a response. I finally texted him again on Monday. He told me that he was injured while playing tennis Friday afternoon and had to go to the emergency room. He needed surgery to repair a torn tendon. I went to visit him at his home that week, which was one of the first times I was at his house. He was sitting on the couch with crutches and a cast on his leg. As we were talking, he unconsciously put his foot up on my leg. It took him awhile to realize what he had done, and he began apologizing and put his foot down on the ground. I felt comfortable around him and took no offense. To me, he was home; it didn't matter. He told me some things that were going on in his life. It was hard to listen to some of his choices but I was listening in love. I offered to make him some of his favorite salsa and he followed me into the kitchen. He stood near me as I assembled the ingredients. He was adorable as he watched me prepare the recipe. Before I left, we prayed together as we often did.

A week later, Bud started physical therapy for his leg and preparation for classes. I offered to wait for him after I taught my class so that he could get a ride home. I knew how much he missed working out so this forced inactivity was definitely a change of pace. I sensed that God wanted to spend more time with him. I gave him a book about renewing the mind by Joyce Meyer. He had read it before and promised to read it again. As I got to know Bud more personally, I learned that he appreciated an auditory approach to learning and did not share my passion of reading for pleasure. He definitely only read what was of interest to him. Just before classes started, he texted me a long message and I knew he was anxious about something. He needed a ride to the Bursar's Office to drop off paperwork, and I let him know I was available to take him. He asked me why I wanted to do that. I told him that I knew he was anxious to get to the Bursar and it was important to me as well. He smiled at me and told me that I 'knew him well.' I did, so very well, and I was still learning all about him. I usually cut through what he said and knew what he really meant. I could tell what he was saying without words. We saw each other at least once or twice a week, and texted daily. He would send good morning messages or I would text him a Scripture. Often, I would send him encouraging songs. One of his favorite songs was "Make Me Over." I did not learn the back story of this song until much later. My heart for this man had grown. He was charming, quiet, sweet, and a joker; yet he had so much pain from his past. Yes, the pain was part of our connection, but I didn't realize this until later. We had an unspoken sharing of familiar childhood trauma. Despite it all, I truly love him.

Into Me You See

One day, I showed him my journal of qualities that I consider necessary in a man. I began to trust him more and allow him inside my heart in a big way. One day, while I was walking with my friend, April, she told me that at some point I should tell him my beliefs about sexuality. This was a terrifying thought, but I knew I had to be honest. I love Bud and all people who have same-sex attraction. The sin is in acting on the attraction. Later on during this journey, I grew in my understanding of how painful this must be. The struggle goes down to the core of one's soul, where wounds fester. My conviction is that God is true to His word. He loves us, but His parameters do not change. His purpose for marriage is between a man and a woman, who in the complementary nature of their union, represent a picture of Christ and His church. Every person has their journey to walk out with God. This subject had to be a point of discussion with Bud, at least once. Bud and I trusted each other. But I did not attempt to have the conversation for a few months. Our relationship was unique, which surprised both of us, truly.

As my connection with Bud deepened, I began to sense how he was doing when he was not with me. We were knit together by God in heart, soul, and spirit. In August 2014, I wept at home as I interceded for Bud. Often, my prayers would become deep sobs without words, led by the Holy Spirit, who led me to pray, sometimes for hours on my knees. Bud told me that he dreamed about me. In some dreams, he had visions of us in elementary schools together. During a time I spent sobbing on the ground with God, I saw my Bible open to Luke 1:45 (NIV), which read, "Blessed is she who believed that the Lord would fulfill His promises to her!" This was in reference to Mary receiving the word about carrying the beloved lifegiving seed of Jesus Christ the Messiah! I felt peace and I had newfound hope in what God was going to do at some point in the future. I could keep going and believe in what God is faithful to fulfill!

God's Abundant Surprises

I began excitedly preparing for a lesson to teach the youth in September on Ecclesiastes 3:1 (KJV): "To everything there is a season, and a time to every purpose under the heaven." I did not get to teach the youth often due to my schedule with work and doctorate work. I was still driving Bud home in the evenings. He had lost weight in his massive muscular legs because he was still recovering from his surgery. I loved him no matter what. I think exercise was a part of his protective factor and hope of a better self-image. I took Bud with me (he was still on crutches) to the youth meeting the night that I was teaching. He was such an amazing supporter! When we came upstairs to the youth room, Bud felt that God wanted him to shake hands with all the youth while on his crutches. I watched him greet everyone, and I saw his pastor's heart of love in the midst of it. Even in his insecurities, in that moment he was following what God asked him to do. Obedience comes from truly loving God and doesn't have anything to do with performance. I loved watching him operate in his gifting.

Whenever I'm going to teach, I always ask the Holy Spirit to lead me. I spoke about sin, the Word. Different colored yarn was used as a visual to show the different paths we can choose to take closer or farther away from God. My yarn became a big twist of different colored strings, and everyone began laughing, including Bud. I was cracking up, too, just enjoying being me. Following the teaching time, Jay, the worship leader, gave a call for anyone who wanted to come back to Jesus Christ. I said to God, "Lord, Bud cannot walk right now to get up there." Well, God humbled me because at that moment, Bud quickly lifted his hand. They were praying for him and my heart was deeply in love with the Lord! Bud's heart was so hopeful to get a touch from God. He was desperate for a touch! I was nearly in tears. God hears our cries! Bud began hugging people around him and Paul Mac, another leader, told me to go and hug him. I went over and he gave me his loving bear hug—such a tight, loving hug from someone I love so dearly. When I wrote about this memory, I cried all over again. I am so thankful God has given me the opportunity to see these moments with Bud, and I cherish these moments in the depths of my heart.

When we were on the way home, Bud was still fixated on his sexual identity, not his identity in God. It is a journey for every child of God to focus on our identity in God, not on any other identity. Later as I began learning more about how human males are designed, I recognize that sexuality holds such an important place in men's thinking, and that this may be why it gets so much focus. When he got home, he asked me to tell his mom about how he raised his hand for new dedication to God, but in retrospect, that was for him. I think he was taught the religion of performance within his church and family. This happens across many families, including my own.

Bud said he intended to come to youth group the next week, but there was an issue in Philly because someone who was gay got beaten. Bud went to Philly while I went to youth group. However, I was praying for him all the time as a covering. I felt led to increase prayers as I got to know Bud more. In October, while on a drive home from class, I finally had the conversation with Bud about homosexuality. The subject came up naturally in conversation and he responded by saying that everyone has a right to an opinion. I know it hurt him and it hurt me to say it, knowing that he had pain. I had deep love for him in all the pain of this situation. It was as if I could see through the surface and see the seeds of beauty inside of Bud that will come out. I just loved the real Bud, that he didn't yet know was there. I enjoyed the person in front of me that was learning how to blossom. Even through the season of this difficult kind of conversation, Bud and I were talking and were still spending time together.

A New Transition

In December 2014, I was at a training session in Harrisburg and saw an encouraging vision from the Lord that made my soul awaken. I kept that vision hidden with joy. The following weekend, I went to the second retreat in the Poconos with the youth. A few months leading up to this time, Devon and Yalli were in transition to leave the church and step down from overseeing youth. The remaining team members were sad and in mourning. One of the other leaders was also transitioning out of youth leadership at the same time. It was interesting because I saw a huge shift in the team morale. This was due to the leadership at the time not allowing the leaders to grieve the transition.

Interestingly, from that point on, the transition of leadership impacted our entire team. Every time I was asked to teach the youth, the leadership asked that I have someone co-teach with me. I discerned the attack on my gift immediately. I love to co-teach, but I was the only person who had to co-teach with a youth every time. Soon after the switch of leadership and shift in the team, it was time for the annual youth leadership retreat.

An Unexpected Realization

On this retreat, more discussion about youth leadership changes occurred. I remember getting up to leave after a difficult conversation about changes in leadership and the youth model. As I did, the one leader got my attention by putting her hand on my arm to speak a word of encouragement. I left the room and went outside abruptly and I began to weep. I knew at that moment God was releasing me from youth ministry. I had come to the mountain with the youth only to recognize my assignment was coming to an end. My heart was devastated and I grieved. A few leaders were coming back to the room and I was crying. I told a few other leaders God confirmed it was time to leave youth ministry. A few weeks later, one of the pastors began asking me to be part of the core leadership team. I said yes. Once I was on this team, I was able to discern that this was not the right fit for me. I had an inner awareness of the leadership's low level of spiritual and emotional health, which grieved me. I also felt restricted as a teacher. Never in my entire life had anyone asked me to co-teach or cast doubt on my strength as a teacher. I began to deeply doubt my abilities. The official step down from youth ministry leadership took me six months of delayed obedience to follow God's original instructions.

New Year's Tradition

Bud and I spent a second New Year's Eve together, bringing in 2015. Once again, we were at the first place we ever went together—the Nightwatch celebration at church. Bud came to pick me up for the evening. Before I got in the car, he asked me how he looked. Honestly, Bud is always handsome and took my breath away. I did not tell him. I was extremely shy with that stuff, especially around someone I adored and deeply loved. I told him he looked fantastic and we drove away. His insecurities were loud at the time. I get it; my insecurities screamed loudly as well, and I am sure he could hear it. Bud knew me so well by now. When we arrived up the stairs to get seats, he thoughtfully found us a place where I could sit at the end of the row. There is something about having breathing room at the end of a row.

For the service, I brought my new purple journal marked with the year 2015. The pastor began preaching about the upcoming new year and making the shift to become holy vessels. At one point he asked people who had desire for great changes to raise their hands. Out of the corner of my eye, I saw Bud raise his hand in desperation. My heart broke into a million pieces for him as we sat there. I did not do the brave thing my heart was yearning to do; reach over and hold his hand. That is who I am today and the love of Jesus would reach out and hold his hand. I did not but I was praying deeply as this moment was silently wrecking me inside. I could relate to Bud's desperation for a fresh touch from God. There were so many changes I needed in my life. We were two people, side by side, in desperate need of transformation. Not just one of us, but both. The service came to an end and we both left, perhaps with some hope and some weariness.

Silent No Longer

Chapter 6

Why can't I find my voice to yell?
Please help me escape from this hell.

Prepared to Speak The Truth

Iapproached 2015 with hope for new joy. Every year, I always write about the triumphs, heartaches, victories, and my goals of the previous year. Journal writing had been a tradition for me since 2012. I journaled whenever I could.

I wrote a journal note to share with Bud to tell him that I loved him deeply. He was my best friend and the love of my life. I was nervous and afraid that I would lose him after sharing my feelings. This revelation was vulnerable and messy, and I had never felt like this before, where I knew someone so deeply without words. There were moments whcre he emotionally shut down, but there was also such unspoken deep love between us.

Snowstorm of Revelation

Bud drove me up to campus in a snowstorm that began during the afternoon. I did not like driving in snow. On that day, I was in the computer lab in my dress-down sweats. He looked over while I was typing and said, "I love you deeply," smiled, and then he kept working. I was smiling inside and kept that memory. After that, I went to the bathroom to cry because I knew I had to share my feelings with him. I got a snack and kept working. He was looking over at me with a smirk on his face as he told me to look down. I had no clue why. When I looked down at my chest, there was a piece of potato on my left boob section of my sweatshirt. I just began laughing and picked it off of my sweatshirt with a quick "thanks." He was still laughing and went back to work. Then we left and he was making jokes as he began cleaning the snow off the car while I sat inside. He said he was "Driving Miss Daisy." We were laughing a lot and I threw a weak snowball at him. As we drove down the road he said, "You are my best friend and the love of my life." Instantly, I laughed, but kept my eyes straight ahead on the road. I did not look to my left or agree with his statement. Those words were right out of my journal and my thoughts, but I left it there. I could have begun to profess my love in that moment, but I was in shock.

We drove on down the road and through the curvy mountaintop. I told him I felt safe with him driving even though I was silently squirming because he kept looking at his phone. We drove down the snowy campus to the city post office. Bud got out of the car, laughing, saying that love is a mystery and he was questioning. I was just observing this whole scene and trying to process it. Bud came back from the post office and got into the car and we headed home. We lived directly down the hill from each other on the same street. While he was driving, I brought up the subject of how he bravely survived the foster care experience. Instantly, he said that it did not happen and it was a lie. I felt a pit punch in my stomach; he acted as if he were experiencing a dissociative shift from post-traumatic stress disorder. The atmosphere in the car felt darker. He finally said he was joking but he was not really in his usual state. The next day, he called me at work. He said his car still smelled of my favorite perfume, "Be Happy" by Clinique, and he thought of me and was glad. He was being so adorable.

Revealing My Heart

As February neared, I knew it was time to tell Bud how I felt about him. I made plans to meet up with him on February 6th. As the time for our meeting drew near, I texted him a reminder of our meeting. His response was that he had to meet later due to completing his work. Bud was often anxious and rigid when working due to a high performance and perfection mindset. But whenever he needed me, I would drop everything to be there for him instantly. Admittedly, this was not the most healthy response. Why? This mindset allowed me to shape how I wanted to be treated by not just Bud but other people. After an hour went by, I texted a counselor friend about how to respond, because I would not be so kind in my response to him without accountability from someone. She gave me a great rationale text to send in reply. After another hour of waiting, he told me we would have to reschedule. My heart sank for several reasons. I was ready to bare my heart to him, but perhaps God knew the timing was not right.

We met the following Friday on February 13th. I did not mention that it was Valentine's Day weekend. I really needed to share my heart. This had nothing to do with the holiday. At the restaurant, Valentine's balloons everywhere. What could I do? I could not tell him how I felt during dinner. We talked the usual conversational points. After dinner, we drove up the hill toward my home where he was to drop me off when I nervously asked him to either come up to my apartment to talk with me or to have a conversation in the car. He listened and slowly began pulling his car over.

The time of sharing my feelings was here. Bud waited as I took out my purple journal. I had rehearsed many times how this scene would look but, nope, it did not look that way in reality. I told Bud that after spending so much time with him I grew to love him. Basically, I was trying to read my journal pages (so classy) the best I could, using the pointers I had in my head and written on a few pages of the journal.

He responded by saying we were friends and he appreciated me; that God was preparing me for my future husband. We talked a bit longer before I got out of the car. When I got inside the house, I felt relief and at peace. Later when Bud got home, he texted me that he loved me so much and that he was not going anywhere and he was here to stay. I wept. My feelings for him were so strong. My heart was full of pain and grief. I spent Saturday processing this and crying.

Bud and I spent time together following the revelation of my feelings for him. I remember telling him the year before that so much would try to break us apart and that we must keep walking together on the path ahead. It was unfortunate that our roads diverged, the paths of our hearts moving independent of each other during the remainder of the year.

A month later in my quiet time with God, He asked me how I would react if Bud began a relationship with someone else. I kept telling God I would be fine. In reality, I was crying; it was a scary thought. God knew the state of Bud's heart and his current state of mind and soul. We would still pray often together. I would later learn that honest prayer together was one of the most intimate acts possible between two people—even more intimate than sex, especially if connected by God. I did not learn that until near the end of our time together. Praying with someone you deeply love and trust is intimate.

Preparation for the Great Defense

Spring was a time of great shifting. One of those shifts was to defend my dissertation! I submitted my final paper to the dissertation committee. After seven arduous years, I was about to finish what I started. My dissertation defense date was scheduled for April 2, 2015.

I invited many of my doctoral friends as well as Bud. Bud was in his first year of the Ph.D. program and was thrilled to be there to support me. He was always telling people how proud he was of me and what an inspiration I was to him with my work.

The Blessing

The day of my defense was special to me. Bud took the day off from work, and I knew a lot of my friends and colleagues at Lehigh University would attend. On the morning of my defense, my friends Allyse and Beth put on my make-up and curled my hair. I felt beautiful for the occasion. I set up my PowerPoint early in Room 220. My co-advisor was planning to call in from Florida that afternoon. On the blackboard, I wrote 3:5-6, for Proverbs 3:5-6, reminding me to trust the Lord. I felt peace. There were at least ten doctoral students attending my defense. Though a smidgen of nervousness lingered, I began to relax. The defense went smoothly, and I was able to answer questions swimmingly. My heart was content and at peace with Bud there in the room supporting me. At times, I made eye contact with him just to stay stable and calm. He may never know what his presence in the room did for me on that day. I am grateful he was still in my life at that time.

The defense was over in about thirty minutes. When I left the room to give space for the committee to deliberate, Bud gave me the hugest hug and then went back to work. I think he was more ecstatic than I was at that moment. Everyone was waiting outside the room, and my advisor came out to bring me back in the room. She said, "Congratulations, Dr. Helman!" All of the doctoral students, along with my dissertation committee, came in cheering. Following this, we had champagne, and my parents came to the room. Dr. Kern thought the defense had went amazingly smoothly. I was so thankful to God that my final defense went so well after a very challenging journey to get there. Dr. Kern told me to submit my dissertation for a special award. I began my celebration with my family and later with one of the doctoral students. It was a joyful day. Bud later sent me a text telling me how proud he was of me in capital letters with exclamation points.

Navigating Disappointment

April was a very difficult and emotional month. My involvement with the youth was on a lifeline and coming to an end. I was preparing to step down officially from youth group within the next few months as things were not improving. God has a way of showing how situations can worsen when you do not listen to His prompting to move on the first time you hear it.

While the youth group transition was occurring, I received more disappointing news. Mid-April, I texted Bud to remind him of my upcoming graduation and celebration party. I was so grateful he was going to be there for me. I asked him to save the date, but he told me he was going to Florida. I did not know it for sure at the time, but somehow I thought deep down the trip must be with someone he might be seeing. I was so upset to hear this news. Bud was defensive at first. I told him I was upset because I was disappointed about the situation and was not mad at him. I understood that he did not have the specific dates.

They Were The Safest Men I Knew

This was a devastating blow to my already hurting heart, nonetheless. What made matters worse was the situation with my beloved Pappy, who said he would not attend my graduation. At the time, my Pappy said that his walking was less steady due to the many surgeries he had on his leg. He also was going through a state of depression as a result of having to use a walker and not always walking like he used to do every day. I also think that my Nana, Pappy, and Aunt Tina did not always appreciate the healthy boundaries I set when I visited. For example, if they were making fun of others or tried to shame me, I would ask them to change the subject or I would choose to leave. Although they respect my boundaries more today, it was not always easy back then. Despite all of this, I believed at the time that my Pappy and Bud were the safest men I knew. I truly felt they were my protectors. My heart had a double blow to it.

The Destruction of My Heart

Later in May, Bud asked me to attend a play with him at a local school. I said that I would go with him, but I learned just before the event a man whom Bud was dating was directing the show. I was stunned. It was only a few months ago that I told him I was in love with him. Did he not hear me? Did he not know how deeply I loved him? Suddenly, I felt as if I was going to throw up. My stomach was in knots, I felt ill, and I could not breathe. After I collected my wits together again I could only text him that "we needed to talk," not always helpful words to say but it was all I could muster in that awful moment. He agreed to meet with me.

I called my best friend, sobbing, trying to think clearly. She encouraged me to not meet because I needed space. After writing and rewriting the text between tears, I sent the text. The result was an avalanche of sobs. Bud responded back stating that he was trusting God that this would all turn around. I did not respond. I could barely breathe.

Gathering Strength to Choose Myself

I loved this man, but I had to choose me. If I let this situation continue, my heart and life would be completely destroyed, more than it was now. This situation reminded me of a verse that truly is relevant to this situation: "The thief does not come except to steal, and to kill, and to destroy. I have come that they may have abundant life, and that they may have it more abundantly" (John 10:10 NKJV). My decision to make a change with Bud was truly life and death for me.

In the midst of the pain and grief with Bud, I was stepping down from youth leadership and I left my church. Simultaneously, my heart was full of disappointment and heartbreak because Bud, my grandparents, and my aunt would not be attending my graduation. Numerous changes in my life were occurring all at once and my heart was in flames.

One week after sending Bud the text about space, I sent him another text before he left for Florida. I told him the truth about what was going on, but I was also choosing to put myself in a battle that only he could complete down the road. I was to intercede without sharing information. My text revealed that I was praying for him and was getting arrows in battle for him on the front lines. While true, I did not need to send him that information. He could not receive or understand it, nor did he respond to me. We both felt rejection and abandonment from each other at some level.

Choosing to leave my relationship with Bud in order to protect my heart from full destruction was one of the hardest decisions I have ever had to make in my entire life. I call him the love of my life. I chose me; I chose God once again. Bud was now in areas of my heart that only God can fill. God had been slowly showing me that Bud had become an idol.

Peace in the Heartbreak

On graduation day, God gave me peace, joy, and love, and I felt no pain that day from all of the recent losses. I had the joy of the Lord inside of me and I was glowing. Family and friends were there in support of me. There were no tears on this day. My friend Christina wrote me a prophecy that this would be a new day and I would smile, waving goodbye to my past. I still cry as I read that bookmark that I have hanging on my refrigerator. By the end of May, I received my doctoral degree, finished my first year as a consultant, and was beginning a new path out of my past. I did not realize the steps ahead would bring me some of the greatest revelation of my deepest heartache and wounds. But God. He had good plans to take all of the mess and weave it together for His good for my life.

The Depths of Heartbreak

Following graduation, my heart was broken and I could barely make it out of bed each day. I felt as if my entire body was aching, in a state of depression, and I was despondent. I felt betrayal, rejection, abandonment, and devalued by Bud. There were days that I remained in bed, barely eating.

This was my first experience of the deep loss of a best friend and love who was still alive. It was deeply painful to grieve a person who was still alive. My soul was aching from the wound. I spent most of May and June reading God's word, crying, and listening to singer Audrey Assad. Her song "You Speak" talks of God healing the heart from a broken love that was second to God's love. I ended up face-down on the floor weeping on many occasions throughout this time. As I look back, I knew God was with me because He is near to those with a broken heart. I was now drawing back to the True Love of my existence; of my entire life on earth and in heaven. I just did not realize how far I had strayed from God.

Summer of 2015 was one of the hardest periods of my life as I tried to get my bearings again after such heartache. In June, I went to see an evangelist named Jonathan Shuttlesworth, who was leading a series of meetings at a local church. He spoke about salvation, deliverance, healing, and the importance of fasting and praying continuously. His words were sharp, but he spoke the truth of God's word with power. After the sermon part of the meeting, he began prophesying over people in the audience. People would fall to the ground under the power of the Holy Spirit. Some people received release from pain.

In my mind, I questioned if this was from God. He asked the entire audience to stand at the end of the evening to receive an infilling of the Holy Spirit. While I waited in line to receive this blessing, I felt a tingling sensation throughout my body from the top of my head to the soles of my feet, as if currents of electricity were flowing through my body. After I got home that evening, I was still questioning if God was behind the healing that appeared to happen during the meeting. I went to see Jonathan Shuttlesworth the next evening, as he was going to be preaching all week. He spoke prophetically again and people were getting healed. I went home late that evening and experienced another filling of the Holy Spirit. My friend Christina came with me the next evening; she grew up in this denominational body of believers. We both went to receive another infilling of the Holy Spirit. I felt waves of the Holy Spirit throughout my body like electricity. It was amazing. I just sat there in awe of God. That night, I woke up around 3 a.m. and heard a voice sounding like many waters say, "It is time, go ye, love the Lord your God with all of your heart, all of your mind, all of your soul, and all of your strength." I was shaken and awestruck to hear the audible voice of the Lord God speak to me!

The next day, I knew I had to go to another session at the church. Jonathan spoke about setting captives free, even in the area of sexual identity. My emotions were still very raw and hurting from the broken relationship with Bud. I sent him a text inviting him to attend that evening but he did not respond. Well, I would probably not have responded to my text, either. In my despair, my message sounded controlling, and if there was anything that Bud despised, it was control. I spent most of the week attending these meetings, searching for God's truth about healing and deliverance. One evening, a friend and her daughter came to the session. Jonathan spoke to her and she went down to the ground under the power of the Holy Spirit. Her daughter was healed from partial deafness in one ear that evening.

The Grieving Process

Near the end of June 2015, I was not eating much and was still grieving the loss of my relationship with Bud. However, we began texting again and made plans to meet up mid-June. I met him at the tennis court since I knew this was one of his favorite sporting activities. My tennis skills are somewhat lacking; in short, I accidentally hit tennis balls outside of the courts, missing cars by mere inches. This was the only time I played tennis outside of requirements during high school gym class (circa 1998). He knew my lack of tennis skills but didn't mention it. I told him that I was just learning and we may not get very far in a game. Rather than starting an actual game, we attempted to hit the ball back and forth consistently. He cheered when we actually were able to hit the tennis ball back and forth more than one round. Later, we walked over to the bleachers, where we ran up the rows across from each other. Let's just be real; Bud was Mr. Track and Field for his high school and college career. He is amazing at running and sprinting. I ran next to him, but sprinting is not an event where I will win gold medals. I think Bud loves this because this is his strength and he can still encourage me. I was in a state of sorrow and, in his mind, I was the thief of his joy. I totally get it; my grief was weighing me down also. When we sat down, I was talking in my sad voice about the state of the world and all of the calamity going on. Bud began doing sit-ups as I spoke about all the sad situations. I didn't send very many texts to Bud after our time together. He didn't reach out, either. The next time we saw each other was before the fall semester at Lehigh. I occasionally spent time with his sister and nieces, but I reduced the amount of time with them that summer to heal. I love those girls and pray for his family all the time.

Falling Into the New Normal

Bud and I both had class on the same night across the hall from each other. He came to say hello to me the first night, mentioning that he hadn't taken any classes in the summer. By the tone of his words, I could tell his heart toward me was different. Later that week, I told his sister that I would drop off some cake to the house for her and the girls. She let me know that Bud would be there to get it. Thud. My heart did a flip-flop at the thought of seeing Bud again. Bud let me inside the house and I offered him a slice of cake. I sat down with him on the couch and we began to talk about many things, including his counseling in groups, particularly with LBTGQ groups. I noticed that summer that he had checked out my Facebook page. He was adding other mutual friends but did not send me a friend request. I think he was waiting for me to send him a request first. I wondered why he didn't take the initiative, but perhaps it was insecurity or being unsure if I would accept. These are my thoughts when Bud does not initiate tasks. I let down my guard and told him I would add him as a friend on Facebook. He was quick to add me as a friend. I was still oblivious about his relationship status. Within hours of adding each other on Facebook, he was liking my recent posts.

When I went to Facebook, I saw his posts about the guy he was dating come up in the newsfeed. The pain from the wounds of rejection, shock, and sadness all resurfaced. That evening, I began a sabbatical from Facebook with the deactivation of my own account. The next day, as I left the classroom during break, I saw him sitting with a group of students outside my class. I had been talking with a student on my way out of the classroom but I instantly became silent when I saw him. I avoided any eye contact. I did not want him to see how hurt I was at the moment, but I felt shame for the rejection. I sensed that he was watching me, but I did not hear his voice as I came out of the room. We were both dealing with mutual rejection. I admit that it had been foolish for me to add him to Facebook knowing what I might possibly see. I had to face the truth about the lifestyle he was involved in, even if it hurt. The initial wounds of rejection for each of us began in childhood, but I didn't know that at the time. The sight of Bud was so painful; I felt a range of intense emotions. I went back into the classroom. We avoided each other as much as possible on Tuesday evenings. Often, we saw each other through the week at school, but there was little text interaction from August through October.

The Healing Journey Begins

My consultant work was picking up in the fall. In October, I went to Las Vegas to present at a national conference. Bud sent me a text while I was in the airport that read, "I miss you." He had been writing a paper and, most likely, was reaching out for support. Hot tears ran down my face as I read it. It took me some time to respond, "I miss you, too." I texted him about some of the things going on in my life that were really dealing with my grief of losing him. I told him that I was in Las Vegas and then sent a very long emotional text message. He did not respond. Bud had said he was there for me. How could I share with the person who hurt me the most? It made no sense to me.

I began attending a class called "Healing Journey" healing with two friends, April and Melissa. This would be an intimate journey with two close friends. I was excited about taking the class, but did not yet fully realize that facing my pain would be part of the process. My emotions were immediately stirred in the first few classes. I had to write a testimony about my life from birth until now, and that has become the foundation of this book. The journey began at just the perfect time for my heart, mind, and soul to begin opening up to God's perfect healing love. Each week, we watched a video and completed a homework assignment to read Scripture and spend time with God about the weekly topic. God often spoke to me during my quiet time with Him throughout the week. The first class was about choosing to believe that God's word is true even when our feelings may tempt us to see things otherwise. Essentially, I can choose whether to believe God's word is true or not. This healing journey addressed my belief system, exposing lies that were hidden in my mind due to pain and wounds. I did a lot of mental processing.

In November, I saw Bud a few times in the hall, but we were not speaking to each other. One evening, I had a dream about him. He was in a room with a man who was on a breathing machine in a comatose state. Bud leaned down near this man. Suddenly, the man awoke and rose up, turning into this glowing, scary-looking blue and silver spirit-thing, which was wearing a white bikini. It rose about 20-30 feet and began to chase Bud down the corridor. It was hovering over him and tormenting him. Bud looked up with great fear as he backed away from it. But despite its menacing attitude, that spirit did not overwhelm him. As he turned his head to look in the other direction, he encountered a woman who was wearing a white bikini. They looked at each other for a long time. During the next part of the dream, I was on a bus in the desert with Bud and other people; he was sitting behind me. I was crying because I wanted to get off the bus to stop somewhere. Bud was focused on going to a club with a man who appeared to be Egyptian. Bud's voice toward me was cold. He did not value me, cherish me, or know my worth.

I realized that dream was about Bud being afraid of women and had to do with an attack on his purity. There were also generational patterns and the spirit of fear and lust running after him. That dream shook me; I remember the details even today. This was one of my clearest dreams. I intercede for Bud daily. One time, I asked God to let me feel his pain, and I was on the ground weeping for hours. It hurt so much. I already had my own pain so why did I ask for his? It was a lesson in praying for others. It also gave me compassion for Bud.

Picking At Current Wounds in A Cycle

In December, Bud and I began texting again. We were slowly rebuilding safety and trust. Deep down, I knew I might not be ready to reintroduce him into my life, but I chose ignorance over God's wisdom. Bud and I had made plans to go to a holiday show in December. The night before the concert, he texted, asking if two of his friends could come with us. Instantly, anxiety and panic rose within me. My immediate thoughts were, "Who is he bringing?" "What if it is this guy he is seeing?" "Would he really bring that guy with him?" "How could he do that to me?" Essentially, it was a train wreck of thoughts driven by fear. Honestly, some of these questions were valid, because I did not see any change of Bud's protection of me. I did not respond that evening so I could give myself time to formulate a response. The next morning, instead of asking him to call me, I just texted him. First, I said that I was not expecting two of his friends to go and that I thought it would be just us. He was trying to understand my response. I still intended to go to the event, but did not realize that miscommunications were still happening because of the woundedness and immaturity in both of us.

I did not realize how much pain and damage this broken relationship had caused between him and me. My heart was shattered, and I was trying to allow him back into my life at a time when I was still healing, which was not at all helpful. I just was so unaware of all the depths of my pain and so was he. I responded that I wasn't sure if I would go to the concert. I had already avoided the straightforward question: Who are you bringing?

In a later text, I told him I felt rejected, shocked, and upset because of the situation. I began questioning our friendship. This was the dark place we had come to after all these events. He was angry and he sent a huge text back to me. I sent him an apology several hours later but it was too late. We did not go to the concert together. I was crying before and after I sent the response. In the "Healing Journey" class, I was learning how to express my feelings rather than stuff them or allow other people to dismiss them. I was done with trash treatment. This may not have been a golden moment for expressing myself; I made many assumptions, but it was a beginning. After reflection, I did see how much pain I was in and how I was not only hurting myself but Bud as well.

I went to my "Healing Journey" class and thought about the situation. I was very upset. I began owning the pain and acknowledging how I was a part of this painful conversation. I had to own my part in this situation with Bud later. I did apologize, with no response from him. He often gave me the silent treatment after uncomfortable exchanges that were frustrating for me and probably for him. He avoided confrontation, yet hard conversations were necessary to build deeper connection. I am not sure if his silent treatment was to avoid conflict or to inflict pain, or both. Or, maybe he was shutting down to all of the emotions of the situation.

The Gift of Surprise with Some Laughter

The hardest part of this situation was my intention to surprise him with meaningful gifts for his 30th birthday. In October, I began to write a monthly prayer devotional for him. This prayer book kept my heart soft toward him in the midst of my pain. I also found important little gifts for him. I bought him thirty little almond joys because he loves this brand of candy. I got him a little toy saxophone because he had childhood dreams of becoming a saxophone player and musician. I also had gift cards for Wings (his favorite) and a water bottle since he always seemed to be without water. A sports themed prayer devotional was in the gift assortment since football is something he loved to watch, the Cowboys in particular (not a fan myself). Finally, I wrote a few prayers for him about the armor of God and included some songs that were important in his journey.

After our disagreement I was so upset but I still had a few more things to get, so I finished getting everything together for his gift. A few days before his birthday, I put everything in a box, put his name on the box and left it on the front porch of his family home. I didn't write my name on the box, because I wanted it to be a surprise. When his mom saw the box, she was nervous because she thought it might be a bomb. She told Bud about the box. He had not responded to me for a few weeks until this moment. I got a text saying, "You know I love you!!!" This was in reference to my text apologizing for the concert we never attended. He asked me if I had put a box on the porch that day. He told me that his mom and sister thought it was a bomb. I had no idea that anyone would think this way (some people have strong imaginations). I told him it was a gift from me for his 30th birthday. He sent me a text early the next morning to thank me for the gifts.

A few days before New Year's Eve, I thought about Bud. We spent the last few years together for New Year's Eve. This was the first year I would spend it without him. Once again, sadness consumed me in the days leading up to New Year's Eve. I thought back to how joyful I felt to spend it with him. This time I spent New Year's Eve watching movies with two of my friends from the Healing Journey. This was exactly the joy that I needed in this hard time.

The Healing Journey was such a surprise for me. I have a special bond with these ladies for life. The journey was part of equipping us for the long run. I had an intense longing to deeply know and love God. The upheaval of my friendship with Bud and all of my emotions put me back into the arms of my Beloved, who is my God. My healing journey process of sorting out my feelings toward Bud began with the realization that I had allowed him to become an idol in my heart. He inhabited the deep parts of my heart that should have been reserved for God alone. It was the hardest surrender for me because of my choice to allow him there in the first place.

During the healing journey, I began to see myself in the story of Hagar. God pursued her after she fled to the desert, pregnant and alone. He saw her when no one else noticed her. He was her comfort; the God who was with her. She called Him "the God who sees me." I related to Hagar because she felt rejected, abandoned, and unworthy. God did not see her this way. He knew her descendants were going to be His children because He knows the beginning from the end. I wept during the weeks of class that focused on Hagar's story.

Another critical week in my walk with God during the healing journey was about judgment. While reading one of the journey questions, when I read the sentence about judgment aloud, I felt as if a sharp knife stabbed through my heart and was stuck inside. I was weeping as I realized how much judgment I held towards others, God, and myself. I was wrong and I repented for these beliefs. I wept and told God I was in pain and could feel the pain of my judgments towards others. This was a necessary moment of awareness and I had a huge piece of humble pie to consume. I spent a lot of time on that lesson, hopefully gaining a heart of humility, mercy, and grace toward myself and others.

Deep Waves of Knowing and Healing

Holy Spirit knew just what I needed on the healing journey, which was to die to the old Amanda and her fleshly ways of thinking and feeling. It was time for a new beginning. The other essential component to my healing awakening was about anger. It was time to get beyond the surface of anger and into the depths of its boiling pot of emotions.

There are seven areas of anger people can have toward God, themselves, and other people. I spent at least two weeks discovering areas in which I had contained deep anger. Some of my hot anger was not outwardly evident. Rather, I had always held it inward, and that was more likely to impede true deep inner healing. Internal anger can impact the body's autoimmune systems and organ health. The long-repressed anger stemming from childhood events was now affecting my body through health disorders decades later in life. I spent time with two women, friends of mine, in the healing journey, processing my hard emotions. I was learning that everyone has a journey, but how deep they choose to go

toward healing depends on their willingness to look reso-
lutely into the mirror and run toward the pain; not to numb
it with outward behaviors that will prevent change. Outward
behavior may look like sexual promiscuity, addictions (food,
sex, drugs, shopping), binging television, excessive alcohol
consumption, and being in relationships to prevent facing
oneself; the list is endless!

The person I was becoming had to keep persever-
ing and traveling through this painful journey. I was slowly
beginning to recognize my lack of self-awareness across all
areas of my life. I spent the whole year with my two friends
navigating this ongoing healing journey with Papa God. The
healing process will cost us everything, but the exchange of
our wounded nature for deep intimacy and knowledge of
God is worth it all. One thing I did was to write a letter to the
little girl I once was who had been so wounded.

Dear little Amanda,

*I want you to know that I must forgive you to set you
free. I know that you were hurt, disappointed and broken-
hearted. You felt so dirty, unworthy, and unloved back then.
Feelings of being unwanted, confused, and helpless led only to
rejection and despondency. Overwhelmed by neglect and abandonment, you felt betrayed by your own abuse of yourself due
to past abuse that hurt you.*

There was a time that I really disliked you and pretty much hated you for everything that I thought you allowed to happen to you and that you allowed to happen to other people. You were fearful, alone, and numb because of the hurt and torment by other people, constantly rejected, and I thought you deserved it because you were never worthy of love or forgiveness. **I never said 'you are beautiful' although it was what you desired most—to be called beautiful, to be loved and cherished, to be heard, to be known, to be seen.** *You couldn't even look at yourself. You hid behind false beliefs about yourself, believed lies about yourself, and allowed yourself to have fantasies that were either super happy, super sad, or super evil or wicked in nature toward others or yourself. Despite all of this anger toward you, I often felt sorry for how you treated yourself and could not move forward.*

I am sorry that you hurt yourself by hiding away all of those years ago in deep pain and sorrow. You were tormented by oppressive voices that condemned you for the very acts that were done to you. You endured too much rejection and bodily harm at an age that you deserved to be protected. **You mattered and what was done to you did matter, sweet young Amanda!** *You were loved by God and it hurt Him to see you run away from Him at such an early age. But you were scared that He would hurt you in the same way. Instead, you began to believe lies about who God was—the trick of deception. You began to distrust God, yourself, and others. Sweet one, in your fear of rejection and abandonment, and the dirtiness, shame, and guilt, you hid yourself away, learning pride and building* *wound upon wound at such an early age. Your fear of talking to others about the abuse and the loss of memory surrounding the abuse were replaced with constant thoughts of unworthiness. This brought a loss of childhood and innocence over the years and false ways to cope with the pain, bringing addictions to thoughts and actions that were not pure and instead harmful to you. Sweet one, your loss of innocence was never your fault and you are now set free from the pain of your past.*

The loss of friends and loss of a healthy mind, heart, and soul was devastating as a little girl. You endured heartache and the shattering of your identity at such a young age. ***You are always worth protection and provision, at an age that should be a time for innocence and healthy development of your identity as a beloved daughter, instead you endured hardship and violation.***

The deepest and most grievous loss was your sexual pureness of innocence. Beautiful little girl, you didn't need to experience anything that would harm you like this at such an early age. It wasn't your fault, little girl. ***God wept with you, loved you, and embraced you when you didn't realize it in your darkest hours and sadness.***

Dear broken girl of the past, I release you to be set free out of your wounded pit, to climb out, run through the fields, and dance with Jesus. Dance away, remembering that He has you in His arms and cleans you up from everything that had you bound in chains. *You are now free of the broken* *past as He restores you. Sweet little girl, you are so loved in Jesus' eyes and heart.* **Jesus had plans to pursue you and save you since before you were born until forever. You are pure as snow, you are forgiven, you are beloved, you are and were always beautiful, you are always worthy of protection and provision, and Jesus Christ has the power to make all things new with restoration.** *Sweet little girl, be free and held in Jesus' arms. You are out of hiding, running to Jesus, and being restored by Jesus as He carries you in His arms as your protector for the rest of your life. Sweet beautiful Amanda, she who must receive love, you are set free in Jesus!*

Come Back, My Love

One day in early January, after journaling about my healing process and thoughts about Bud, I received a text from him wanting to meet with me. I asked God to show me the exact time to meet that week. Bud responded later that we could meet on Sunday. I was fasting and praying that weekend and planned to attend the local house of prayer event that Saturday.

This was a new experience for me. I didn't know much about this event so on my way to the house of prayer, I asked God to show me where the building was for the prayer room, since I never been there before. If He led me there, I said I would go inside. I was praying as I drove down the street trying to find it and saw the building. Next, I told God I would go in if someone else drove into the parking lot. A car came into the lot. I then said to God that if I could not get into the building I would leave. I had met the girl I saw in the car, in front of the building. She was headed into the prayer room. I knew I should go in there because God had answered each prayer. I sat down in the house of prayer and began to pray. Less than ten minutes into the prayer session, the leader asked people who were under 40 years old to come up front. I knew I was to go up front. I stood in a line where the leader began praying for commissioning to go to the Middle East. My feet were there but one foot was close to running out of the room. What? Had God brought me here to tell me He was going to send me to the nations? I remember the lady who said a prayer for me. It was a supernatural moment. God was planting those seeds for a date in the future. After the prayer, I walked back to my seat and I sat down again. A woman came to me and said that the eye of the Lord searches for those who love Him. She recognized that I was on fire for God and that my heart was turning toward Him and that He desired for me to pursue Him. Truly, I knew that I had been divided and left my first love, Lord God, for earthly loves of men and it did not satisfy. I was crying and knew my heart was turning back to Him. I felt His love pour deeply into me that day. The great thing about this moment was that a few weeks earlier, I was able to open my heart to God's love and receive His love for me. I began to glow with the realization of His love and pursuit of my heart. I was glowing from basking in God's deep love for me. A change came over me that weekend.

The next day, Bud text me, and we decided to meet at Starbucks. He suggested we meet at On the Border, but I did not feel that would be a healthy place to communicate due to the noise and large crowd of people. He really was just thinking about salsa and chips since he loves Mexican food. Looking back, yeah, I think he was just about the food.

I really wanted to talk with him about our last miscommunication and misunderstanding. I was fasting but I did not tell him. Bud hoped that I would travel closer to where he was living, but I requested that he meet me halfway since it was raining. I read my Bible while I waited for him at Starbucks. I was asking God to lead our conversation. I saw a picture of grapes behind me when I turned around. This gave me hope because my favorite movie was *The Song*. A scene from the film shows the wife telling her son in front of her husband: "You do not want to spray the grapes too quickly. It may cause them not to grow as they should. Treat them right and they will let you know when they are ready." I saw the grapes as a symbol of hope between Bud and me, perhaps representing reconciliation.

When Bud came inside the cafe he gave me a quick hug. I raved about the grape picture. He chuckled, said the word grapes, and went to purchase a drink. When he sat down, I began talking a lot because I was nervous. Bud took notice that I was glowing; he has a strong prophetic gifting. I told him about my time with God.

Honest Communication Tangled with Pain

We began to talk about the communication mishap between us. First, he said "thank you" for the gifts I gave him. He said that the meaningful gifts did touch his heart and were relevant to his life. I told him I was very anxious the day of the concert because I was unsure about who was coming with him. He asked me why I didn't say something about it on the day of our miscommunication. He was trying to understand what was going on with me because of my response. Bud often did try to understand me, but I did not see it that way.

The next part of our conversation became a lesson I had to learn about when to share prophetic dreams. I told Bud about a dream I had with a big demonic presence chasing him. I said it felt like a mix of fear and purity. He listened, as I had once told him I had a dream of him with flies coming out of his mouth. He listened even more intently. I did not realize at the time that this kind of dream should only be revealed as God guides, in order to provide encouragement whenever possible. I was still in the learning process of revealing prophetic words.

I loved the man across the table from me. He was someone that I could read instantaneously and he knew it. He could read me as well. He told me he had been ready to walk away from our friendship. I was listening to him. I was learning so much more about how to listen well. At times I struggled to listen because I was so busy protecting myself, which was always my barrier with him. He had moved through a lot of my walls, but I kept my self-protection wall up at times with him. He did the same. He told me that God said that we would be together in later years. I wondered if he was being honest. A man should not tell a woman something like that unless he believes it to be true. I just sat there and said not a word after he said that to me.

Then the conversation began to turn as we laughed together. Several hours went by as we talked. Before we knew it, Starbucks was closing. We prayed for each other before we left. He held my hands and prayed. It had been a tough season of separation and pain but now, here we were at Starbucks, praying together eight months later.

I told him I would pray for him next. Before praying, I asked Bud if I could put my hand on his heart. I always felt led to honor him. He said yes. I can remember his heart beat to this day. He took my other hand and placed both of his hands over my hand. I asked the Holy Spirit to speak through me. I began by blessing him as a man of God. When Bud hears something empowering, he says "hmm" as it hits home to him. I remember this bittersweet moment with Bud and cherish it. I felt that we had achieved some measure of reconciliation. While walking to our cars, he became my hero by figuring out how to start my car by using the remote. I began squealing with joy as he looked at me with intrigue.

That week, Bud was preparing for an interview with the VA office for an internship in Philadelphia. I sent a text to him in the morning on Wednesday, to let him know that I was praying for him. He was just in prayer when I text him and thanked me for praying. While we were at the coffee shop, he had spoken about his anger, and it was part of my prayer that he would be able to process those emotions and seek God about the underlying causes of the anger. I sent him some words of encouragement, which he appreciated. I prayed for Bud many times, whenever I thought of him. He said I should come to Philly with him to explore the city. I had work to do that day; otherwise I would have been there with him during the interview.

The Sound of Silence

After that day, we didn't text again for months and everything went silent again. I was waiting for him to text me, to see if he was going to put in the effort to remain in touch with me. He did not take initiative and I was shifting in my response to him. Our relationship was inconsistent—on and off, hot and cold—and I did not want to be in the position of putting effort into our interactions if it wasn't reciprocated. His lack of initiative and effort to keep in touch hurt me. However, this revealed the current state of his heart and his pain.

A few months later, I was driving down the road near my house, praying for Bud. As I came up to a stop sign, Bud was driving by and paused before turning down the street towards his home; so did I. We made eye contact for a moment. I was so sad to see someone I dearly loved from a distance; this hurt my heart deeply. His car turned left and I turned right down a different street, our actions representative of how we were moving in different directions relationally. My decision was to keep moving forward despite my deep love for Bud. I was allowing God into all parts of my heart and I was learning how to love myself. I saw Bud a few times that year at Lehigh, and we said "hello."

Some California Healing

Through several months of grieving my relationship with Bud, a friend and I planned a trip to California! The plan was to fly there then drive down the coast. One of the reasons for this trip was to celebrate my doctoral degree. On that trip, I began to recognize how sensitive I was to the different land regions. When I set foot in San Francisco, I could feel different types of regional, territorial, and spiritual atmospheres.

My hopes of getting a dark tan in the California sun were quickly dashed as I realized most parts of northern California had a cooler climate, even in the summer. We went to a few beaches wearing long sleeve shirts. The first place we stayed was in San Bernardino, about an hour outside of Los Angeles. Fortunately, the nearest car rental to where we stayed in San Bernardino was close to the most amazing burrito place, which was the best kept secret in the area.

After a night there, we drove the entire coastline to Santa Monica Beach for the day. While on the pier, we stopped at my favorite Mexican place, which has amazing margaritas and hot salsa with chips, all with an excellent view of the ocean. Following the trip to Los Angeles, we explored a few different beaches that I had missed visiting a few years earlier, due to the forest fires. I really had a challenging time when we were traveling through San Francisco and Los Angeles; I could feel such a sense of the spirit of death and suicide. My sensitivity to the land continued all the way to southern San Diego.

Before the trip, I asked God to show me a way to serve Him while I was away. One night while we were out at a bar in downtown San Diego, I noticed a man coming out of the restaurant towards us. He appeared devastated. He was drawn toward our table and said hello. He sat down and began to talk to April and me about his life. I listened quietly. We said a prayer for him as we left that place.

Can You Run Further with Me?

While I was jogging alone one day on Coronado Beach, God told me to keep running beyond my original goal. I began to cry as I ran. My run led to a place along the beach that was empty of people. It was just the sand, sun, ocean, God, and me. The tears continued to stream down my face. God was inviting me to move forward in my relationship with Him, but He was also telling me I would have to let go of some things in the process. I spent more time in the sun before returning back to the hotel.

When I returned to the room, I logged into Facebook. I am sure Bud had seen the new pictures of my current trip. That weekend, my friend April helped me get dressed up for a fun night out in San Diego. That evening, I decided to unfriend Bud. I felt torn over this decision.

Releasing Shame

After my return from California, I attended a conference at a local apostolic center. One lady came up to me and told me I was beautiful. I had tears in my eyes as I said, "thank you." Later, a man named Richie was going to speak. Immediately, he felt God was planning to break shame off of people. My eyes glanced down to peek at Christine Caine's book, *Unashamed*, that was in my lap. I told God the sign for me to walk up to the front of the room was for me to cry. I sat there but nothing happened. Deep down, I knew I had to get up and move my feet. Often, God meets me once I get up and move toward Him. Yes, God could come to me, but there is humility in going to meet Him! As soon as I stood up and I began walking down the aisle, hot tears fell down my face. I walked to the front of the room and began weeping on the floor.

Richie began to speak. I did not know it but his mom stood beside me. She was crying and told me I was like the woman at the well. She told me that God loves me and I was not disqualified based on my past. Just then, Richie began to talk about the woman at the well. I began to sob all the more. A woman next to me told me that I would be like a magnet for those with mental health issues. God was restoring all of my health but one of the biggest areas of His redemption was my mental health. I hadn't quite realized all this while at the conference but I was seeking God more than anything in my life. Shame left that day and I walked back to my seat feeling so much freer and lighter.

I hope that I never stop running up to the altar to God, or in any place for that matter alone or in front of others, when I need Him. Even as a leader, may I never be too prideful to hold back from running in desperation to the One who is my great Physician. We all need our Papa. Someone else prayed over me that day and I was willing to receive impartation of spiritual gifts. Richie later declared joy over me. The next day at church, people noticed the change in my demeanor. It was invigorating to boldly speak to everyone that morning about what God had done for me the day before!

Yes! Yes!....No. The Waves of the Heart

At the conference, Richie also spoke about becoming friends with the Holy Spirit. While driving from the conference that evening, I laughed and asked Holy Spirit if His favorite color was blue and if He loved cheesesteaks. I did not hear a response. After church the next morning, and the whole day, I went around forgiving people, including my parents. I was alive in the Holy Spirit. My next stop was to get coffee at a local shop on campus. When I got out of my car, I halted. Bud's car was parked a few spots down from my car. I said, "No, God." I did not know what God would ask of me concerning Bud, but I was still raw with grief. I walked into the coffee shop and noticed him at a table with his back toward me. He did not see me. I quickly bolted out of the shop, got in the car, and began driving around the block. Holy Spirit had other plans for me to encounter Bud.

I went to campus the next day to finish up some work. I put my belongings in the computer lab and then left the room to run some errands. I was wearing my beautiful new blue sun dress that day. One of the administrative assistants complimented me on my new dress. I thanked her and then proceeded to walk into the computer lab. Bud was sitting at the computer he usually chose to do his work. I did not see him yesterday but was glad God had us meet up today! Bud told me that as soon as I came into the room his headache left and he felt peace! Thank you, Lord! He said he texted me to see if I was around. He came over and put his hands on my shoulders to massage them, like he sometimes used to do. He sat down and offered to move closer. He acted like a high school guy with a crush (which was cute), and I said he could move down to sit closer to me if he wished. He took a look at me and told me he was going to text me. I just smiled and said yes. In his text, he said I looked beautiful. Although he was two seats away, he texted me instead of joining me where I sat. His text made my heart smile. I thanked him. Later, we were helping each other with our work. We were an excellent team with complementary strengths. I told him about my time at the conference and what God did for me. He listened. I also told him about how I wanted to go in to see him at the coffee shop. Bud said I should have walked over and said hello. I also told him how God was calling me to forgive people and I was struggling with having to forgive myself and Bud. He was cracking up at my questions to Holy Spirit about His favorite color and cheesesteaks. I miss Bud's laugh so much sometimes. I was constantly learning grace and humility from Bud. He has given me tremendous grace at times despite my emotional rollercoaster and healing process. This was a very different season for me and I was in constant search of God.

Silent No Longer

Chapter 7

I fear stating such darkness everyone will leave me.
Can you look past the pain and see me?

New Connections

I met Kelsey, a professional counselor, during my time at a local church. After I left that church, I was still in connection with her. She had sent me information about Bear Creek Ranch ministries. After I had a vision with her in it, I contacted her about counseling. She gave me some advice about where to look for a reliable counselor. Before leaving the church, one of the men began to prophecy that I would have rivers of living water flow from me, but that soul wounds were preventing this river from springing forth. He also prophesied that God was working with me. I spent some time in the remaining months of 2016 contemplating what was next in my life.

In December 2016, I joined with a local church to help serve dinner to homeless people. My tears were flowing as the kings and queens, as I call them, walked into the room because I felt such love for them.

It was once again a quiet New Year's Eve, but I did not mind that. I had purchased a new journal and reflected on my year, which was one of my favorite things to spring into the new. I began 2017 delving into my pain and into more transition. I was part of a Bible study group focused on how to stay free after deep healing journeys. I know clinging to Jesus Christ is the best way to remain free. I'm thankful for what God was doing.

In January 2017, I signed up for a prophetic deliverance and inner healing retreat. I wanted to get rid of any block in my walk with the Lord. As the date drew closer, I decided to drive down there because it would be cheaper, and I would be able to spend some time at Virginia Beach both on the way down and back up the coast. The retreat was scheduled for April 7th through April 9th, 2017.

The Fullness of the Promise

I left on a Wednesday evening and arrived late at a hotel in Virginia Beach. I slept for a few hours and woke up early so I could visit the beach before traveling down the coast. This trip was a special time with the Lord God. I was heading toward a kind of freedom I had not known was possible. I arrived at the retreat center just before noon on Friday. I was so nervous to enter the building. Once inside, I checked in, got my workbook, and found a seat up in the front of the room. I felt awkward not knowing what to expect, but here I was, alone in a group of other people who were probably thinking similar thoughts. I had begun praying from the time I checked in at the hotel room and I was asking the Holy Spirit to fill me; my desire was to be completely free. That evening, in the corner of the hotel room, I saw little green lights that looked like fireflies flying in the corner of the room. I felt peace around me, but it was an odd sensation to see these little one-inch glowing bugs flying around. I woke up early the next day to make sure I arrived on time for my prophetic deliverance session at 8 a.m. As I got seated before the session, I saw a picture of my heart. In the heart, I saw a woman crying, saying that nobody loved her. She was sitting on the ground weeping. The picture began to clear, and I then saw a picture of a bright blue butterfly. As the session started, I heard confirmation of the vision I had seen, and I was in tears. I felt naked immediately after everything was gone, but I was finally free of spiritual oppression. I received a new infilling of the Holy Spirit. The one leader walked me out to another room for prayer. During the prayer time, I was told that it looked like somebody took a match and set my heart completely on fire. I was grieving and in pain. I sat for a while, crying and allowing myself to feel the pain. As soon as I was delivered, I heard so many voices; the voices of my soul wounds. The experience was unsettling. I became afraid that everything demonic would return. But I no longer had the old sense of feeling unlovable. I felt such a release of my entire being. I spent the day processing my new-found liberty in the Holy Spirit. I had not known that all saints need deliverance at salvation; the need is critical. Then, inner healing begins and is ongoing. The strongholds in one's life are hidden by these attachments. I am sad that so many people do not receive deliverance. An unclean spirit is a lying spirit that does not want you to know that you need deliverance. Jesus Christ demonstrated the greatest model of casting out attachments from disciples or with others throughout his ministry. In fact, entire cities were at the door with sickness, disease, and unclean spirits. This indicates why deliverance is necessary for all people who believe and follow Jesus Christ. The deliverance process does not have to be a dishonoring event, either. Deliverance is the bread for God's children, but unfortunately, some have made it into a spectacle or an abusive event.

Back at the hotel, I saw one of the trainees. He told me he was praying for us that evening. I was so grateful. I grabbed a book with a blue butterfly on the cover called *Shelter from Abuse*. It was the same blue butterfly with some black lines that was in the vision I had prior to the deliverance. There were lessons in the book for survivors of sexual trauma and guidance as to how to navigate through the healing process. I purchased that book during one of the breaks at the retreat. After the last session of the retreat, I drove back to the hotel in Virginia Beach and went to bed early.

The Most Painful Darkest Wound Revealed

That evening, I felt unsettled in my soul. I kept seeing images of someone who should have been a safe person all of my life and I began to cry. For the past two years, I had been remembering weird images of this person and had some questioning thoughts about my childhood. Until this moment, I did not want to face what my body already knew. I was a survivor of sexual trauma at the hands of someone who should have protected me the most. When I finally chose to admit this hard truth, my entire body began to shake and I curled up into a fetal position. I wept for hours in the darkness of my hotel room.

I was terrified to face this painful truth that was hidden for over three decades. I can only remember a few little details of the sexual trauma, and there may have been other wounds; but this one shredded my entire heart as a little girl. It was hidden away into my subconscious for years. In this moment, I felt frightened, shocked, and full of heartache.

Now that the deliverance was completed, I had to face the beginning process of healing my deepest core wound. I texted a friend late at night to tell them I was having a difficult night, but I felt God's presence with me as He held me all night. The next morning, I went to breakfast and ate three to four Krispy Kreme donuts. This donut habit had been gradually changing on a deep level, but at that moment, I was shamelessly numbing the pain. I grew up trying to numb my emotions by eating, but it only made me feel worse. I ate to self-protect, but I was now learning about how to allow God to protect me. I felt naked and exposed, and I was so sad that morning. I decided to take the last donut and head out to the beach.

While walking along the beach, I began sobbing while mustering some words to cry out to Lord God. My heart was broken by the revelation that someone so close to me didn't protect me but chose to violate me. He had a desire to protect, but he never kept his word. My heart was aching to be close to Jesus Christ so very greatly. I told God I did not know how to begin this healing process and that I needed Him so much. As soon as I spoke, I began drifting closer to the waves as they crashed inland. I began to laugh when big waves hit my pants legs. God was encouraging me to laugh with him amidst the utter disparity.

I had spent a lifetime seeking people who were safe and secure. I realized it was difficult for me to find people who were safe, but I unwittingly sought out men who had no idea how to be protectors. I was always trying to find my father. I could not understand this as deeply at the time, but Lord God is my perfect Father and He protects me at all times. One of the hard questions I was navigating was what happened during the abuse and where Jesus Christ was through this terrible event. He would show me later when I was ready to hear and see it. I will explain this more later.

After leaving the beach early in the morning, I began the long drive back home. I called my friend April and wept on the phone as I told her the revelation. I was in so much pain and heartbreak. As I drove, I was praying for angel armies to be in the car with me and Jesus. Now, the inner healing would begin. That next day, I was on my way to teach my reading class in the evening. I felt as if my entire being hurt from the great spiritual surgery I had that weekend. I made it to class on time but felt like I had been hit by a massive truck. I was sore, broken, and in great need of rest. It was by the grace of God that I was able to teach class that evening.

I told my friend Kelcy what God began showing me after my deliverance. She met with me one afternoon and recommended that I go see a counselor for support. God knew who to recommend in that season. In May, I went to a wonderful counselor whom I adore. I would process everything with her bi-weekly. While in counseling, I was also going through the Healing Journey class as a co-leader in the fall. It was painful to reveal this information to those closest to me. I began journaling about my pain and the sense of betrayal I felt toward this person. In May, God began revealing other details. The sexual trauma did not occur only with me but within my family. I made the connections through my entire life history and remembering family interactions. No one would really want to face that. I also began learning generational family sexual trauma patterns. Family patterns, on both sides, revealed forms of sexually, emotionally, verbally, and physically abusive family members.

I grieved about my own abuse but also about my entire family's abuse, and I did not want to continue in this vein. In a conversation with God, I told Him that I would allow Him into all of my mind, heart, and soul to remove any residue of these past generational patterns. That month, I had a dream that the enemy was trying to shoot arrows at my head that would cause me to fall off a mountain. *The healing of my mind was critical to my entire health and well-being.* This revelation was difficult to carry, knowing I could not share it with my family but only a select few people whom I trusted. I spent the next few weeks trying to navigate the immense pain. I began to experience panic attacks in the evening, before bedtime. My chest would hurt and I felt as if I could not breathe. The panic attacks reminded me of former times when I went to bed and felt suffocated to the point that I could not breathe. I had some flashbacks, and although I did not know how to process all of my pain very well, at least I was willing to try. I asked Papa God to help me heal all of my soul wounds; I read Scriptures and wrote in my journal about my pain.

Saying Goodbye to a Dear Friend

In the mix of navigating through my painful revelation. I heard that a former client was very ill. Jay was one of the men I had spent a lot of time with in my job working at the group home.

I took Jay to church once, on Easter weekend. The speaker that day was talking about a time when he did not think that God could love him. Jay asked, "God doesn't love him?" I said, "Jay, he thought that, but God does love him!" Jay nodded silently. I enjoyed spending time with Jay, but when I used to work night shift, he would often yell for someone to help him. And as he was aging, he would call for his mother. There is no record of sexual abuse in Jay's history, but he may have been a survivor of abuse. Jay had frequent nightmares. I would come to his side and let him know that he was all right and safe. I had also gone through a challenging time with Jay after his incredible roommate passed away suddenly from a heart attack a year earlier.

When I heard the news, I reached out to Bud and told him that I was going to visit Jay since he was ill. Bud had said that he would come with me to see Jay, but did not show up at the time we had planned to go, so I went in on my own. When I arrived at the home, I could see in Jay's eyes that he was getting ready to go home to the Lord and the time was near. With tears in my eyes, I began to read to him from the card I brought. I prayed for his transition to heaven, gave him a huge hug, and then just sat with him for a while. I finally left, grieving him already.

Two weeks later, Jay passed away. I thought Bud had gone to see him on his own, but that did not happen. I heard later that Bud was deeply upset that he had not seen Jay before his death. Jay meant a lot to Bud and I knew it. I knew he was grieving and I prayed for him as I always did but more specifically in this situation.

Marathons of Preparation

In 2017, I started to train for a half marathon set for September 2017. While training, I had no idea how much

stress and toxins were in my body from all of the trauma
and abuse. My body was showing signs that it needed to heal
from the inside out. Running has always been a joy for me.
Sometimes I run both long and short distances. This year,
my hip was in great pain. An MRI scan showed bursitis. The
doctor wondered if I had my thyroid tested during the visit.
I did not. My thyroid level was at 40. A normal thyroid is at
a level 0 to .5. Due to hypothyroidism, I had to stop training
for the half marathon. With hypothyroidism, it is possible to
gain weight even while exercising, if your body is not getting what it needs to work properly. I was gaining weight
while running, which is truly absurd. In fact, once my body
had the necessary elements to balance my thyroid, I lost 20
pounds in less than two weeks. That was wild!

After several months, I was able to work out again
and had some success with a plan I was working on with a
local chiropractor. However, the cost for a chiropractor truly
out-weighed the health benefits in that case.

One positive outcome of the chiropractic visits was
to learn the types of foods to eat to heal the thyroid. During
chiropractic visits, I also had tests to assess hormone levels
and identify allergens. Fortunately, I did not have any heavy
metals in my bloodstream. I was feeling better that year as I
pursued an ongoing process of thyroid support. The thyroid
level went from a 40 to a 10, still not normal, but better.

Food does impact the thyroid as some foods are
highly inflammatory. I have learned how to avoid eating to

compensate for painful emotions and to turn to God as my comforter instead. Food is a source of fuel for the body but there's such a temptation to use it to provide comfort; but that idea is a counterfeit resource. I have grown so much that nutrition and mindset is a priority of my life. At times, frustration ensued at the slow changes occurring in my physical body even with different healthy eating habits. I stopped drinking soda and I was eating nourishing foods. However, year after year, I would promise God that I would take a year to really eat differently but then I would feel like a failure when it wasn't perfect or I didn't see changes. I put so much effort and striving on this area of my life rather than learning from what He was showing me.

Another Great Loss Of Life

In June 2017, I planned to go with my siblings to Las Vegas but the weather forecast was storm and hurricane warnings. That summer, my cat, Kiki, became ill. She was vomiting a lot. Three weeks before we were supposed to leave, I took her to the vet. I did not think to check to see if she was going to the bathroom as she never had any problems before this time. The vet felt her organs and said they felt normal, and her blood tests came back normal, too. I took her home with some medicine. She did better that day. I gave her the white medicine, but later that evening, she threw up again. I was crying because she was ill, and I did not have the money to take her back to the vet as I was going to Las Vegas with my siblings. It was painful to watch her suffer and my mom was nervous to watch her during this time.

The next day, my brother spoke with me out of concern for Kiki. Instantly, I began sobbing, telling him that everything was too much right now. In my distress, I told him that I was in counseling, I just could not keep everything together. My brother usually calls me and I just had no one to support me at the time. It was another intense moment in my life. After that day, Kiki kept hanging on although she was getting weaker. I did not know that pets try to stay alive for you. I loved my Kiki with all my heart. Later that afternoon, I found a vet who does house calls. I was ready for Kiki to be done with her suffering, so I found a time for the vet to do the euthanasia procedure that afternoon. The vet was kind and gentle as I pet Kiki and looked her in the eyes until she passed. After the vet left, I cradled Kiki in my arms and took her to my parent's home, where my dad agreed to bury her in the yard. I came back to my apartment and cried. My other two cats were quiet and sad. They knew Kiki was not coming back home.

Road Trip to Lake George

My siblings and I canceled the trip to Las Vegas and planned to drive to Lake George, New York, instead. I picked up my sister at the Philadelphia airport. After dinner, we began searching for a hotel nearby, but could not find a safe location. We then drove to Newark, NJ, later that evening, to pick up my brother. I offered to drive on to New York, because I was the only one who slept a full night's sleep in the past 24 hours.

The next day, we spent the afternoon at a festival downtown, and in the evening, we went on water rides with water guns. We had so much fun, and the experience was healing for all of us, as we laughed and made memories. My sister wanted to go hiking the next day. We had to park at a random entrance and climbed up stairs to walk across a questionable bridge over the highway. We had lots of laughs and began to follow the path up the mountain. I took a glance around when we reached the top of the hill, where I heard crows cawing. I began praying for us in Jesus' name. My sister looked back at me and asked if I was pronouncing a curse because she felt a push while walking. I was in shock due to this accusation. I serve a loving God and I am a woman of God who prays that curses would be broken and that blessings would fill the atmosphere. I felt as if the enemy was feeding her lies. As an intercessor, I felt a strong urge to pray for our safety throughout the walk down the hill. My siblings moved on ahead of me and my sister, at first, was asking me to stop praying. I didn't respond, but continued praying under my breath. Prayer is a good first response to any need. We were working through healing that trip. This was the first time on a trip with family members that I didn't have my old attachments. I'm sure it changed the trip dynamics. Overall, we had a great time together as family.

Watching A Revelation Unfold

After my sister flew back to Wisconsin, my brother remained in PA for a while. During the week, I asked him to stay with me at the Hershey Lodge. One night, we began to talk. My brother and sister both had revelations about painful abuse that happened to all of us. It was an avalanche of emotions to work through, but we all felt that we understood each other better because of this sad epiphany. The minute the body and the mind make the connection to the root of abuse it brings brokenness.

Admitting a broken nature allows deep healing light to enter into our minds, hearts, and souls.

Dating Events

Earlier that year, I had gone on several dates with a guy nine years younger than I. He knew a family friend and so we met up at Bar Manwell. Our dating spree was short as we were in different places on life's journey. He would reach out to me from time to time until I chose to delete his number. I also met a guy that got his graduate degree from Lehigh. We began talking on Facebook and then met up late one night at Bar Manwell. I nearly made mistakes with this man due to not keeping my own boundaries. I had to explain my current beliefs to him. That same week, I felt led by Papa God to delete the contact information of all the men with whom I had ever had any type of a physical relationship. I was ready for a clean slate.

Summer Mandela Fellowship

Meanwhile, I was hosting Mandela Fellows from all over Africa through a global program at the university. One of my greatest blessings was meeting my friend Emma. She and other members of the Mandela group attended a get-together at the house of a friend who hosted a fellowship meeting on Sundays. One of the guys, John, from the Mandela group began talking to me in a friendly way. I met him later on one afternoon for lunch. As I talked about my faith in Jesus Christ, I was pleased to discover that he was also a believer! I was cracking up! He would text me, asking to visit my place. When he told me my husband was 'down the road,' that made me cry. As soon as he said it, my thoughts went immediately to Bud, who lives close by. I never realized, until that moment, that his house is on the hillside opposite from mine. John continued to contact me after he returned to Africa. I think he was trying to get me to go to Ethiopia. If I had gone, I'm not sure he would have let me leave! When I tried to set boundaries on appropriate hours for phone calls, he began calling me in the middle of the night! Granted, Ethiopia is seven hours ahead of our time zone, but I would have thought he was aware of that. I had a dream about a predatory spider one night after a phone conversation with him. I heard his voice in my dream and I knew this man was not the one for me. I broke off the relationship after that. In the midst of the healing process, I was finally learning to love myself.

Partial Reconciliation in the Lab

Near the end of August, I donned my new workout outfit and went to the Lehigh computer lab with my combination purse/gym bag. Bud came into the lab soon afterward and sat down at one of the computers. Bud asked me if I lost a sock. I looked over and started laughing as I rose out of my seat. I said with a smirk, "Yes, I did! I am now going to do the walk of shame to get my sock." We began roaring with laughter. I think Bud never knew what to expect from me. I didn't either, sometimes, but I was feeling lighter these days. I had socks in my bag and I guess one sock jumped out near Bud's seat. I'm glad God has a sense of humor. That little comical moment broke the ice and made us feel more at ease. We began talking about other humorous things. After we had talked for a while, we did work.

Before I prepared to leave for the day, I remembered the blessing prayer I had recently learned that honored a person's past, present and future self. I asked Bud if he wanted to pray the blessing prayer with me. I said we should stand to do this. His body language showed a little uneasiness at first. He stood up and faced me. I explained to him the blessing prayer model. The model was for the two people to hold hands, look the other person in the eyes and bless their good and difficult life events. I took the first turn, in order to model. I looked into his eyes and blessed him in his childhood, telling him he had been brave in the pain and trauma. I spoke blessings over the little boy who went through separation from his family, and I ended with a blessing over his struggles and the development of humility. When it was his turn, he blessed me in my childhood, knowing the difficult situation with my father. He blessed me for my gifts and where God was leading me. I was about to leave after the prayer, but felt led to tell him about the new revelation I had about the tremendous sexual abuse I had been through. He listened closely as I told him everything. I wouldn't cry in front of him. I wanted to appear strong. He gave me a long hug. I whispered in his ear that this was healing. He just held me. As I left the lab, I was glad that, once again, Bud and I had reconnected.

Second Round of the Healing Journey

In September, my friend and I began co-leading an inner healing study with women, She was a certified trainer and I was taking it again because it was essential to my healing and wholeness. I also chose to sign up for the advanced wholeness retreat. I was on my way to Cartersville, GA. I made it a few hours and had much to learn. The hardest part of the lesson was learning who I am and how to identify my core false belief.

In the evening, I sat in the hotel room asking God what my core false belief was and started to write a list. I wanted to find the root of the matter, no pun intended. Why a pun? Usually core beliefs are a punch to the gut. Each person has one or more core beliefs, often some branches of beliefs but one main root. If not dealt with, the core belief will surface with little punches to the gut in a variety of circumstances.

The next afternoon, I was at the advanced wholeness session. One of the facilitators had each of us share our core belief. I said I had a few and could not narrow it down. The facilitator began asking me if I was willing to allow the Holy Spirit into my soul and I said yes. As he spoke, he said something that made me get to the root of the matter. In doing so, I began to weep and put my head face down in my lap. Before I did this, I saw pitch black darkness. He had everyone leave the room except for the women and his wife and daughter, both facilitators. I kept weeping as the women gathered around me.

After crying for a few minutes, I picked up my head. I said that I felt like a traitor and felt condemnation. At the time, I felt inadequate. My false core belief was that I was not good enough since it was painful to say out loud and brought me deep pain. The following day, the ending activity was about love. It was an amazing deeper revelation of a kingdom of God concept. I really went through some painful processing with the Lord and it felt good to move through the pain.

Pain is not easy to face but once you get through it there is joy and relief. Before I left, I took time to thank the facilitators. The facilitator said my vulnerability within the group would help me achieve deeper wholeness. This means going deeper into core issues in order to receive emotional release. He then asked me to find out if there was a deeper core belief that I had to face. I remembered what he said as I drove out to Atlanta that evening. During the night, I began asking the Holy Spirit to show me what I really believed about myself. Instantly, I remembered my time at the retreat and I saw the picture of the black darkness. Then the realization hit me. I knew this was the deepest belief because I wept despondently. My core belief was "I am darkness" and I am unworthy of love. Specifically, my belief is that I am not worthy to love myself or worthy of receiving love from others. I had a hard time receiving love and affirmations of my worth. This was at the pit of my deepest sorrow. Another similar belief was that all I could expect was pain and darkness. This mindset is kingdom-of-darkness thinking. Perhaps this began after the childhood trauma and abuse. I think it was also a link to generational patterns. It took me all week to process my true belief system. I chose to continue on the deep journey into the soul wounds that Lord God was showing me because I was asking for soul health. I wanted the deeper freedom, so I acknowledged it, and continued to plow deep until all the old unhealthy roots were gone.

Pride often gets in the way of healing deeply and it can cause an attitude of denial that there is anything going on. Based on my knowledge prior to deliverance, I had no idea of the great need for deliverance after salvation. However, after I became part of a prophetic team of people who went through the same process, I wanted to help others to get free. My hope is for everyone to realize what the Scriptures say about deliverance.

The issue is that unclean spirits are also lying spirits. How many believers, even with the Holy Spirit, will be able to admit they need deliverance unless they realize they have both light and dark? The dark is the demonic attachment. Matthew 11:35-36. I just continue to share my experience and pray for people to recognize the need for deliverance, as they witness deeper freedom in those who have gone through prophetic deliverance. Of course, deliverance can occur anywhere the Lord sovereignly chooses, but believers need to know it is possible and necessary part of the process.

Revelation of the Impact of Childhood Trauma

A few weeks after the retreat, I facilitated a presentation at Penn State in the area of early childhood transition. While at the conference, I sat down with a lady who spoke to me about an early childhood trauma presentation session held after lunch. I chose to attend that session, too. In fact, something within me knew I was to attend this next session.

The presenter began to discuss trauma and the ACES (Adverse Childhood Experiences Survey). She gave an explanation about the higher score of an ACE score associated with the increase in health risks in the future. I was curious and took the entire survey. I had a high score of 8 out of 10. According to this, the trajectory of my physical, mental, and emotional health was looking grim for the future. I cried as I realized this. After this difficult yet important session, I went upstairs to cry and process the information. I missed the next session because I was a mess, emotionally. It took me a few hours to process my emotions and return for other sessions. While processing the information, my hope held that as a daughter of God, along with having access to more knowledge and wisdom from Him comes healing and a catapult in the opposite direction.

The next conference session began to fan the flame for my passion and boldness in stepping out into the area of mental health and trauma awareness. This was my lifelong story. It was Papa God's love for me and His love and light within me that took me out of deep pits of darkness into His healing light and freedom. I gave Him a "yes," and went deep into the emotional processing. I give God all the credit for my being able to become who I am today.

Similar Paths

Soon after the conference, I had planned to meet up with Bud at one of the campus labs. He was working with people in the area of academic work. Now, his work included men who were survivors of sexual trauma at his internship. I began to see how God was shifting him into an area where he could work, in but also provide an opportunity for him to glean deeper answers when he was ready. God had shown me deeper revelations about Bud's childhood that I never told him about because it was between Bud and God to work through. I hope I will be in his life when he does process everything, but I also pray that he has other people who can support him if I am not to be part of his healing process.

While in the computer lab, I asked Bud if he knew about the ACES study. I asked him if he had taken the ACES survey. He quickly said he had not taken it. I recognized his avoidance. People who are studying to be a counselor usually have an interest in taking that survey, unless they suspect it will be painful or jar something within them that they are not ready to face. I said nothing and put it away.

New Opportunities

I applied for a job as a consultant at the state level. I knew that it may be a stretch as they were searching for a speech, language and autism consultant. I had my first interview in the middle of April. It went well, but in my nervousness, I probably spoke more than necessary at the completion of the interview. A few days later, I got an email asking me for a second interview.

My second interview was quite interesting. I overheard some of the interviewers question why they were there for the interview. One person noted they did not feel like being present. I do not believe this impacted the interview but I was more nervous than usual for it. In retrospect, I still did not value myself. Today, I would have addressed the group, thanked them for having me, but I would not have interviewed out of my own self-respect.

A New Year of Hope

That New Year's Eve, I wrote in my journal and I spent time in reflection about the whole year. This is my favorite event when the new year occurs. I was also asking God to help me fully let go of Bud. This was quite a feat for me. Whenever I came to the place where I would tell God I was letting go of him, we would end up seeing each other. When I prayed, I would say prayers to bless him and to break ungodly soul ties by the blood of Jesus. My heart still was drawn to his at times.

In January, I was to give a presentation at Spoken Word, an art poetry spoken on stage by a variety of performers. Participants can speak about various topics. When a line has a powerful effect, the audience will snap their fingers to show their appreciation. Before I wrote my own Spoken Word, I was encouraged by two of my friends who spoke at the Spoken Word. I was amazed to watch these two supposedly quiet women come alive on the stage. A few months prior I wrote two pieces to process my pain of discovering the deeper revelation of my childhood abuse. One of my friends read the poems for me. I have a penchant for rhyming. I sent my two pieces to the founder of Spoken Word. He read both pieces and said I could be part of the lineup. I was so very excited, yet nervous. I was about to speak the truth about my deepest pain on a stage in front of unknown people. This is true vulnerability and nakedness to bear one's soul and pain, yet so relatable. Some of my closest friends attended. One friend was going to read the second piece on stage with me. I arrived an hour early, as requested.

The line-up featured new and old poets. My time on the stage was during the first half of the show. Some of the poets had written amazing lyrics and sang beautifully. I was stunned as I watched people from all backgrounds share stories of humor, pain, highs, lows, fears, sadness, grief, anger, joy, and disappointment. The show was raw and real. Sometimes I cried, and other times I almost fell to the floor, laughing hysterically. When my turn came, I went up to the stage. Each poet had to select a piece of background music. The founder introduced me, and then I climbed the stairs and walked to the microphone with my phone in hand. I did not memorize this piece; it was on my phone, although I knew it well. I saw the crowd of about 250 people, and even though I had friends there for support, I could not see anyone's eyes. When I began to speak, you could hear a pin drop. Everyone listened silently as I spoke of my pain and my redemption. The next piece, I spoke with a friend. I went downstairs after I read the two poems with a huge smile across my face. This was the first time I had ever told my life story in front of an audience. **In that moment, I felt set free to speak!** There was nothing holding my voice back! I felt so free to speak on such a difficult topic as abuse. I hugged all of my friends.

Set Free

"I would like to take you on a journey about me. You see, I got stuck at age three. It happened when I went through drastic abuse that froze my identity.

At age three, I became a shell and hollow. I would go where anyone would lead and follow. I had so much pain and sorrow.

At age three, a little girl was abused by a man who she desired to call protector. Instead, he chose to be a lecturer. She hid those memories deep inside. That pretty little three-year-old girl had nowhere to hide.

Three years of age, she felt hopeless and broken. It hurts to not understand why you feel so closed and not open.

That little girl felt dirty, ugly, and numb. She already accepted the false identity that she was dumb. Her head hung low and she would never show—her beauty. She desired to be loved but was thrown and shoved.

That little girl grew up rejected and unaccepted. By everyone most of her life. She cried out to God and lived life in strife.

That little girl ached to be called princess and Cinderella. She gave up herself to the wrong type of fellas. For awhile, she yearned to be loved by a King. Instead, she chose to get caught up in men who would only sting—her heart.

Silent No Longer

It took years of living to please others—for her to discover— that she was worthy. Decades later, this girl was tired of feeling dirty.

She finally wanted to know who she really was—cause—everywhere she went people were trying to tell her she was a lost cause.

One day she got so tired and was there, but not really. She got to a point even she knew was scary. She was so tired of rejecting the design God gave her—she didn't know how to get back to the way He beautifully and perfectly made her.

One day she finally fell to her knees crying out to Jesus, her Lord and Savior. As she wept with those she loved she never felt braver.

That little girl in the pit finally started to get up. Shine. She knew it was time. Her lost identity began when she wholeheartedly surrendered to the Divine. Love of Lord Jesus, who was simply her Shine. He taught her love, kindness, and all about serving. She only didn't know she was deserving of all of it.

In her quest for a King, she settled for paupers. Now, knowing the greatest love of her life, nothing will stop her.

Lord Jesus picked up all of the broken pieces and put her together in His presence. She finally learned what it meant to rest in Him.

She now knows her true identity—a daughter of the King. She will stop at nothing—to let others know the same thing. Beloved, you are beautiful, worthy and valuable. Never let anybody call you laughable. Your identity is in the Creator. You are well loved and have favor. May you be set free—becoming the person you were called to be. This true freedom is for you and for me. May you become all that you were designed to be- Free!

Who are you?

I am the darkness that hides from the pain.

I want to say all is fine to hide the stain.

Who are you?

I want to get out of this pit.
Why is it so dark and I can't sit?

Who are you?

Why have I allowed darkness as an identity?

Why can't I get out of this disparity?

Who are you?

Why does fear, shame and guilt surround me?

Silent No Longer

Why can't I just be free?

Who are you?

Why am I surrounded by my own condemnation?

Why is the darkness such tribulation?

Why did I allow unworthiness and harm to surround me?

Why did this three-year-old girl die inside me?

Who are you?

I see darkness and anger and evil all around me.

I sit in this dark prison cell.
I don't know if you want me to tell.
Why can't I find my voice to yell?

Please help me escape from this hell.

Who are you?
I fear stating such darkness everyone will leave me.

Can you look past the pain and see me?

Who are you?

Lord Jesus, I believe You exist in my heart.

Lord Jesus, I feel that I am so apart.

From You.

Who are you?

Lord Jesus, I want to get out of this prison.

I just know there has to be a reason.

Who are you?

Lord Jesus, it's coming near me please help me.

I cry out in distress desperately.

Who are you?

Lord Jesus, I see You and Your light
Jesus, why are You bending near me to ask me if I am alright?

How is it You can understand my plight?

Who are you?

This little three-year-old girl cried out, she's alive.

You are bringing her out of this cave of darkness and she
doesn't have to strive. It's You who is her power—it is You who
saves her in her darkest hour.

Silent No Longer

Who are you?

This little girl is crying out loud.

In You she sees You so proud—of her tiptoeing to You for help and love and light.

Who are you?
I am scared to come near the light.

Lord Jesus, I am done resisting, please hold me tight.

Lord Jesus, please show me the way out and fill me with Your light.
Who are you?

Lord Jesus I need You every second.

You are King of my Heart and I never want to be apart.

Lord Jesus, why didn't I come closer to You?

Lord Jesus, You never left me and everything that hurt me, hurt You, too.

Lord Jesus, teach me how to hear You.

Who are you?

Lord Jesus, Your voice is getting clearer.

Lord Jesus, I want to draw nearer.

Who are you?

Lord Jesus, the enemy's lies of false identity are falling.

Lord Jesus, I am willing to hear You calling.

The deepest core false beliefs and lies

Are now the false beliefs I despise—as light fills me with

Your truth

About who You are and who I am in YOU

Who are you?
Lord Jesus, I see You bright in Your glory.

Lord Jesus, are You sure You want me to share my story?

Who are you?

Lord Jesus, I am darkness who died to self and turned to nothing,

It is I who gave You my shame and guilt and condemnation for Your blood covering so that You, Lord Jesus, in me can shine light to expel darkness

And lead others to know You are marvelous

Who are you?
I am free in my identity in Christ.

I am love, I am light, I am a daughter of the King, it is Jesus' light that expels the darkness in me that makes me sing.

Sing again, sing loud. Thankful, humble, leaving the old for the new.
I am no longer the girl I once knew. I am singing and dancing in the light.

I will bring light and darkness will flee at the name of and the sight of Jesus Christ of Nazareth, Son of the Living God.

Fully Set Free to Fly

The New Year of 2018 brought so many emotions as I began to shift into deeper healing. I had resolved to move forward and fully let go of the relationship with Bud, but I ended up texting him a couple of weeks into the new year. He did not respond. There were moments when I really missed him and wished I could be with him. However, the timing was not right. In a deep way, I was beginning to apprehend my true identity, but Bud was headed down a different path. He once told me I was worthy, but the words were empty without actions to back them up. I had a painful time letting go of all of the hopes and dreams in my heart concerning Bud. I could not imagine my future life without him. My heart was beginning a healing process to recover from a deep and painful wound. I remember telling him that the road ahead was going to be hard for both of us and that we shouldn't give up on each other. He agreed.

I kept working on my children's book. In March, Bud and I texted briefly, and last text he sent made me sad. I could tell that his heart had changed toward me. I had to cement my resolve to move on and I would only text Bud to see how he was doing after I experienced nights of intense prayer and dreams. I knew not to reach out often, but I continued to pray for him with all my heart.

Near the end of February, I flew to Georgia for a prophetic deliverance training weekend. The first meetings outlined procedures for helping with the deliverance sessions, but I had a huge headache and felt apprehensive about the whole idea of taking the training. I was beginning to doubt my gifting and the calling on my life. Confidence is the opposite of doubt. I know, intellectually, that my confidence cannot be rooted in my own strength, but in the power of Holy Spirit, who is living inside me. When the time came to participate in the prophetic team deliverances, I wasn't sure I had anything to contribute, but I asked the Father for an exchange of my natural perceptions for the mind of Christ. I needed to be sure of my identity and the One Who provides liberty to the captives—Holy Spirit! The sessions went well and I knew that I the Lord was prompting me to go back later for more training. During the debriefing time, I was able to share what God had done for me, with the new group of people who had just been set free.

I am still grappling with the idea that we (believers, and the church as a whole) are not really preparing the saints with the full benefits of the work of Jesus Christ at salvation. I am alarmed to think that most believing saints of Jesus Christ seem to be limping in the darkness they call 'sin,' and are unaware that they are really being oppressed by demonic attachments. A person can have all the inner healing possible but until the removal of the ruling spirit, they will continue to be subjected to unhealthy influences in their lives. Yes, the process of inner healing is deep, challenging work. Removing the pressure of these attachments allows a person's entire soul to become full of light in the Holy Spirit.

A Shift in Calling

After I returned from my trip, I began to prepare for an interview with the trauma-counseling program in Philadelphia. The interview went well and I had peace about my soon-to-be involvement in the program.

A day later, an email appeared with a letter of acceptance from the university. The program began in the fall of 2018. Immediately, I knew this was the beginning of my shift toward a field that I had been interested in before, but at that time I felt extremely unqualified. Despite this hesitation, a small spark of enthusiasm for trauma healing kindled in my heart. I had no idea how much I was to learn in the years ahead.

Another beginning point in my life was when I applied for a position at a local shelter for women who were survivors of human sex trafficking and exploitation. I received an email from the director of the shelter in March, inviting me to visit the home. I drove to the hidden location and met with the women. I sat at a table with them and we played games. Some of the women began to open up and talk while others were quieter. I really enjoyed interacting with them that evening. Later that week, the director told me that I was a great fit for the program. I spent several evenings with the women during a two-week period and then I began my new position at the beginning of April. Based on my experiences as a supervisor for people with disabilities in a home setting, I recognized both situations had similarities. The similarity is that the frontal cortex, or the center for executive functioning skills, is greatly impacted. The difference is that the cause and effects on the frontal cortex and executive functioning skills differs and manifests differently. For example, people with disabilities have impact on their cognitive functioning and/or social and communication. Social communication is impacted for those who experience trauma but it is due to different experiences and horrific events that impact the mind-body due to unwanted trauma that is sexual in nature. The women had varying trauma-based wounds due to trafficking. Unfortunately, many women sold in trafficking already have an abusive background of emotional, physical, or sexual trauma. Those women with the greatest wounds seem to be the ones that traffickers target and enslave. This evil commerce is appalling and inhumane. I spent the first week painting fingernails and getting to know the women. We spent time getting to know each other during many evenings, since they knew the other woman that I was replacing extremely well. I stayed overnight at the home twice. That summer, I spent a considerable number of hours at the home. I felt their emotional pain, so that was a challenge for me to deal with. I also have a high level of spiritual discernment and my dreams revealed the torment they experienced daily.

Some Unexpected Healing Breakthroughs

I didn't have a good understanding of a work hazard called, "compassion fatigue" at the time. Working with the women weekly brought up painful issues that I myself was still navigating. I was part of the Bethlehem Healing Room's team and they were offering advanced training that I realized I needed. Fortunately, God knows what we need in our healing process. A licensed professional counselor was scheduled to teach about how to release the pain of emotional trauma. At the beginning of the session, the speaker asked people to raise their hands if they had need of prayer. I raised my hand, but he didn't call me up front. He demonstrated the emotional trauma release model with one of my dear friends. Next, he demonstrated again with another woman who was able to release her emotional trauma as well.

Near the end of the training, he remembered that I had raised my hand earlier and he asked me to come up front, with a friend standing behind me for support. What began as a simple identification of anxiety escalated into a huge state of panic—I saw black. He realized that I had deep trauma. Once again, my vulnerability was on display (I was wailing), but I was able to release that pain from a deep place within. After the session, I felt peace in my mind and body; this was such a contrast to the incredibly strong anxiety I had felt in my mind, body and soul prior to this release. I began thanking God for this relief and wanted to continue the process of breaking free from my soul wounds. The next day, the counselor who had led the seminar came over to me and spoke many words of affirmation. He encouraged me to continue the healing process, because he sensed that God was going to collaborate with me in a mighty way. I later gave a testimony of how different I felt after releasing this emotional trauma; but in the following days I knew that deeper healing was necessary for what was ahead in my life. I emailed the counselor to schedule a follow-up session. He was supportive in helping me through the process of releasing some deeper levels of emotional trauma.

Of All Possibilities...

In the middle of the summer, the community trauma counseling program offered graduate students the opportunity to volunteer at their annual conference. As a volunteer, I could learn the campus layout and attend presentations, which was also a way to meet the professors and students.

One morning as I was driving, on my way to volunteer at the Philly conference, I looked around and saw Bud in the car behind me! Out of all of the people driving between Bethlehem and Philly, our paths crossed yet again! Perhaps he didn't see me—or maybe he did. At one point, our two cars were side by side. I did not look his way because I was certain of his plan to ignore me; at any rate, I was ahead of him until the rain started. I chuckled to myself, because Bud drives the speed limit. I sometimes enjoy a little extra speed when I drive. All of a sudden, I saw him speed ahead, and then he was ahead of me. That drive to Philly was definitely an interesting trip. And, to this day, I know that he saw me then, but neither of us reached out to acknowledge it.

Fall 2018 was a busy time: I was working with the women survivors of exploitation, continuing my consulting job, teaching a class at Lehigh, taking classes for administrative certification, and also taking two counseling classes in Philly. This combination of activity made for a somewhat hectic existence. However, I was learning to pray for protection and strength before, during and after every visit to the home.

One of my first experiences in the community trauma counseling program was when I was placed in a group with two women who were practicing witches. One other lady in the group, a Muslim, eventually became a friend. During the first class, I overhead one of the practicing witches talking about how she put curses on people. Hearing this made my stomach turn. The woman had some understanding of spiritual realms, but she was using counterfeit power for evil purposes. I was interested to listen to her talk with her friend who was also a practicing witch. My classes took place every other week for a period of eight hours. The next weekend, the class had to pick topics for discussion. I began praying, asking God who He was going to put in my group. I sat at a table with women who were practicing different religions, and we discussed various topics. In that first class, I faced fears that God was helping me get rid of entirely. God is the only One who is Creator and is to be feared. There is no room for fear of any false god or secondary creation. God is omnipresent, all powerful, almighty, omnipotent and yet always loving. He was teaching me to rest in and rely on Him.

Taking On Too Much

That Fall, as time progressed, I knew I was involved in too much. During the week, I worked overnight shifts, getting minimal sleep due to the great need of prayer at the home; I was also taking courses, teaching courses and intentionally focusing on my own healing. By October, there was one woman at the home, a new director in the process of arriving, and some staff leaving. I knew, for my own mental health, that it was time to step down from the Truth home.

My love for the women at the home deeply knit my heart with theirs. I gave my notice with the intent to stay for an additional month at the home. After I left, I felt peaceful, knowing it was time to press deeper into Papa God for more healing. Working with women in trauma was still a little too close to home for me. I began pressing into Papa God to release my own ongoing emotional trauma.

A Bushel of Surprises

In December, classes began wrapping up for the semester, in anticipation of the winter holiday break. My sister was making a surprise visit home to plan a celebration for my mom's 60th birthday. My brother was also planning to come home for the holidays and for my mom's birthday celebration.

Once my siblings were home, we began planning the celebration with my dad. My dad found a delightful space at a local restaurant. We ordered a cake, found balloons and decorations, and followed up with guests to confirm attendance. The celebration was scheduled to take place two days after Christmas. Amazingly, none of my family members accidentally said anything about the surprise birthday, even while together for the holiday dinner. The next few days, we began finalizing plans for my mom's birthday celebration. We were so delighted to see mom's appreciation of celebrating her special day early. Her face lit up and she went around happily making conversation with everyone in the room.

State of the Heart Check

Following the party, I gave my sister a ride home. As we neared the house, my sister and I began to discuss the party, but soon, the conversation began to shift to other topics. I listened, appalled, as my sister became very upset and said that she was more easily triggered by me than by my dad. The words painfully shot through my heart like pure sharp arrows. I sat and listened to her until she hurried out of the car. As I drove away, hot tears began to stream down my face and drip down my shirt onto my lap. I cried all the way home.

I was very upset to hear that my sister dreaded facing me more than facing my dad. She also said that I was particularly challenging that day and I had not changed a bit. I got home and ran to Papa God in tears. I was in despair. I spent the whole evening talking with God about this matter. I was so hurt to hear my sister say that I hadn't changed, when I knew very well that I had made so much progress. I was also asking God to search my heart to see if I was to blame in this current situation. I was feeling pain and condemnation. In the morning, my heart felt very sad indeed, and I heard the word 'condemning.' After crying and processing, I drove to the prayer room. Upon arrival into the prayer room, I lay prostrate, face down on the floor, weeping and crying out to God. I was so despondent and sad. I asked God for forgiveness for my own sins and any responsibility I had in the situation from the other evening.

Later, I went to a local store with my friend April, and I wanted to get some feedback from her about the details of the hurtful exchange between me and my sister. My goal was to be accountable and receive input and correction. After our discussion, she suggested that the enemy was using this situation to bring condemnation. The idea that I had not grown spiritually was a lie. I am still a work in progress but God has brought me through such an amazing transformation process, and He continues to do so. After we talked, I was able to compose text messages to both my siblings, but I allowed my friend to read them first, in order to ensure that my words were loving, yet truthful. I am a private person, but I do seek God's counsel and confirm it with facts and the guidance of a trusted friend. I felt peaceful after sending the messages. Part of me was sad because that evening I had been expecting to spend time with my cousins and my sister. However, I respected my sister by giving her space. In some way, I was glad she had spoken about painful matters from the past; I just felt so hurt by the way she spoke of it. But I was able to extend grace and love to her and accept her current place in her own healing journey.

Cousin Time

Later, my sister texted me back and apologized, saying that she realized she said things that were not true. She invited me to come over and play family games, but I chose not to go. I said I would come out with them and our cousins later that evening. I really enjoyed spending time with them. I left early that evening as they wanted to also visit some other places that evening. That night was a night to remember. The next day, I spent some time with family. Then my friend Beth and I put the finishing touches on the children's book that we had been working on all year. This was so exciting! The most challenging part was getting the formatting just right. I had to spend a few hours learning how to reconfigure the book! I turned in the final copy on New Year's Eve! Publishing my first children's book was the best way to bring in 2019! My siblings were both planning to return home later that evening, and I had planned to head to the beach. I had lunch with my family at my Nana's home. She made corned beef with mashed potatoes, and corn, a family tradition, for New Year's Eve. I hugged everyone and drove to the beach late in the afternoon.

A Beach Trip for the New Year

I was thrilled to head to one of the places I greatly treasure for a new year! I was staying at a cute bed and breakfast with a breathtaking view of the ocean in New Jersey. A light drizzle was falling when I arrived. I went up to my room and immediately hurried outside onto the porch to look at the view. The sound of the ocean was so delightful and peaceful, and the temperature was not too cold. I went to get some food at an Italian eatery nearby and brought half of it back to the beach house, a block away from the ocean. I began writing in my journal. I was so pleased to find such a room for New Year's Eve.

Every year since 2012 I had been journaling events of my life story. On New Year's Eve I would reflect on the past year and review dreams that were in the beginning stages, examine areas of disappointments, growth, hopes, and goals for all areas of my life.

Some goals take longer to achieve than expected because it takes time to get to the deep roots of belief systems. I define progress as one step at a time. Progress also requires a change in how you think. Changing the patterns of how you think may take time depending on how many years, or decades, you have allowed unhealthy thought patterns to exist.

A deep inner-healing journey begins with the will to navigate through difficult issues of the heart, mind, or soul, in order to identify the origins of unhealthy deeply-rooted patterns of thought and behavior. Transformation begins once a person chooses to uproot any lies or false beliefs formed due to trauma or hurt. For me, the extraction of a deep root must have an exchange. I give the roots, lies, false beliefs, painful feelings and emotions to God and process them with Him. After those emotions are released, I then receive something from Him as a replacement, such as peace, joy, love, or a vision. God is so very loving and amazing in that way. I give him my junk and He gives me something much better than what I relinquished to Him. I serve an amazing God! I just want to love God and serve Him as He loves and serves me. I want to be loyal to Him and be transformed because He is my Creator and Papa who loves me!

I spent the evening on the porch outside of my room. I had a delightful time. I began processing some intense emotions with God and then I gratefully went to bed early that evening. In the morning, I journaled some more, praying and reading God's word and thanking God for this year. I like to begin the year this way. I saw a video that suggested praying Psalm 1 every day and singing it. I love to sing to the Lord. After that, I went down to the second floor to have breakfast on the enclosed terrace overlooking the beach. January 1, 2019 was a beautiful sunny day with temperatures in the 60s, so I decided to walk the beach after the delicious meal. The weather was so lovely outside and I felt so thankful. God knew this was the beginning of a wonderful year!

It's Time for a New Adventure

I was off to a conference in Harrisburg by the end of the week, where I picked up an information packet about a global missions trip. I asked God where he was going to send me to minister in the nations. I love to ask God questions and open my Bible. Sometimes He surprises me with what is next. The pamphlet was open to the page containing Pemba, Mozambique. Africa! Yes, Lord! On the left side of the page, I saw the name, "Wood." I had heard something a year ago about a man with that last name. I knew God sent me His confirmation. I was filled with delight! I began to ask God to strengthen me in fasting and prayer and listened for His responses.

Silent No Longer

Chapter 8

Sing again, sing loud. Thankful, humble, leaving the old for the new. I am no longer the girl I once knew.

Write Your Story, Beloved

I prayed at home for God to restore my brain and integrate its parts. A few weeks later, as I was in the prayer room, I knew God was healing my brain because I could feel a significant difference since I received prayer. He has been faithful to keep restoring and redeeming me because I am His own daughter. Since 2003, my walk with the Lord has been growing. He was doing rapid and incredible work within me over the past five years. In the prayer room, my friend Kay gave me a prophetic word, stating that God was asking me to write about my journey. I was excited about this, because I had already been journaling about my inner healing and deliverance experiences over the years, even from childhood. God was going to honor me and glorify His name through this process of writing a book about my journey with Him! He said now that I have a sound mind, I must stop listening to the enemy. (That struck a chord with me!) God gave me a sound mind and when God tells me to do something, I do it because God the Creator is the wisest One of all! My eyes began to fill with tears at the thought of all God was going to do in my life. I was so thankful, and I really believed Him. He also reminded me of my teaching gift. I always want to know more from God.

The next day, on January 19, 2019, I obeyed Him and began writing the outline of this book. The official start of my book-writing began on January 26. I felt amazed, knowing God had been planning this book all along. He is my most beloved Friend and Redeemer. I had begun writing but was not sure how all this was going to work out. I felt vulnerable at the thought of publishing my entire story because it would include the revelation of sexual abuse that happened at an early age that kept me hiding in shame my whole life. I prayed and asked God how to go about this type of writing. My decision was to plow ahead and trust that He was working behind the scenes. My desire is to honor God first and my family second. I can trust God to make everything work for good in intricate ways, because He IS good. I was thrilled to begin writing creatively once again. Creative artistry is part of who I am!

Use Your Voice

The beginning of March was the first time I was going to teach through Ekballo Harvest, Bethlehem Healing

Rooms, of which I was a part. I had always prayed for the Lord to keep me hidden as He was building my character and integrity as a woman of God. I had prepared a teaching that was my heart's desire and passion; it was simple to understand, but isn't that the gospel and good news? The message was: *"Come to the Lord God and allow Him to love you, transform you, and empower you to serve, love and honor Him and His wonderful name forever!"* However, we often lose our childlike faith due to disappointments, heartaches, or comparison. Under a spirit of religion, we often hinder others that God is drawing to Himself, people who want to come forward, seeking more depth of relationship with God. Since I have been delivered, I often chuckle because some people who despise religion are often blind to the fact that they still have a religious spirit, which is a tricky concept. A person can try to go far away from it and still unknowingly retain the residue of what they didn't like about it. Enough said. Deliverance and inner healing is key for removal of the religious spirit.

The following week I prepared to go to Florida! I was wanted to stand with over 60,000 believers of Jesus Christ in the Orlando, Florida, stadium. I was planning to stay with my friend, Danielle, who I met at Bear Creek Ranch. Danielle is an amazing woman of God. She picked me up at the airport. February was bearable with the realization of sunny Florida in my near future! I arrived on a Thursday night. Danielle and I stayed up late talking and praying. The next evening we went to Disney World! We had so much fun on the rides and walking around. I bought some salsa and guacamole for us and Danielle also had a box of snacks. We walked eleven miles across two different parks that day.

We woke up the next morning to participate in The Send, a gathering of followers of Jesus Christ hoping to impact the nations. Danielle and I met up with two of my friends, Trina and Edie, and they drove us to the stadium. We were so excited to see so many believers getting ready to go inside and worship Jesus Christ. We were there early to get good seats into the stadium. While waiting outside, Trina and Edie began to pray for some of the people around us waiting in line.

As we were waiting, people with large signs began protesting the event. Their thinking seemed to be based in a spirit of religion. Holy Spirit, at one point, led me to talk with one of the women. I asked how she was doing and whether she wanted a hug. She asked me if I was going inside the stadium and when I answered, yes, she said she was unable to accept a hug. This is a form of conditional love, which says something like: "If you do this, then I will love you." It is not true love. God promises to love us no matter what and He is there for us, but our choices and our own misunderstanding of Who He is cause barriers that keep us from drawing closer to His pure love.

One of my favorite memories of the event was hearing Tasha Cobbs sing some powerful songs and give some prophecies from the Lord. I heard testimonies, some of which broke my heart and others that gave me hope and made me grateful for God's faithfulness and goodness. Gratitude is a choice. As the meetings concluded, Danielle came back and I met some of her friends. Her pastor saw my superman t-shirt and commented that I was a strong super woman. Yes, thanks to the Lord! Danielle asked some of her friends to pray for me. They spoke prophetic words over me that I knew were true. I transcribed them into my journal to remember for the days ahead. Later, we saw a young man receive a word from the Lord that he would be going to the east coast. We were amazed to see his surprise at the accuracy of the Lord's word for him. At the end of the evening, Trina and Edie went to the stadium. Originally, pastors were supposed to pray for the people on the stadium field. However, flexibility is key in these moments. We were close to the field and the presence of God was strong. I began to allow a deep surrender of myself to the Lord.

All of a sudden, I had my hand on my belly and my arm in the air. My arm began moving and I did not intellectualize it. I just went with the flow of the Holy Spirit. My legs began to feel hot and tingly as if I were running in place. I was experiencing the Holy Spirit in an electric manner that I had never felt before in my life. I was awestruck and so thankful for this encounter with God. At one point, I almost fell backwards as the wind of the Holy Spirit began pouring over me in waves. Later, as the event was ending, I was still soaking in the Lord's goodness.

The next day, Danielle and I went to Clearview, Florida, where we enjoyed a beautiful afternoon sunbathing on the beach, but once we hit the road again, rain began pelting the car. We were thankful for yet another amazing day and perfect timing in weather. When we returned to Pennsylvania, the bitterly cold weather came as somewhat of a shock after beautiful, sunny Florida.

Months of Unexpected Surprises

A few weeks later, I received a call from a publishing company, which I didn't answer; but as I was listening to the message, I told the Lord that when I returned the call, if a live person answered, I would know this was from Him. When I called, a real person answered, offering me an opportunity to display my book at an event in Los Angeles in April. I knew this was something I had to do in faith. I spoke with my illustrator, who was a little unsure, but we ended up agreeing to pay half to put the book on display. I made arrangements to head out to Los Angeles that April. One of my friends from my counseling program was going to go with me. I was so excited! In March, I wrote a blog and got an offer to speak on a radio show connected to this publishing company. There was a fee for the radio show, but I knew this was not the time.

I thought of sending Bud a copy of my book. I had been asking God about this for several weeks. I was hesitant, because I knew moving on from this relationship was critical and necessary. Growth meant that I would be moving forward. I had already given a copy of the book to his sister and the girls, including a special note with my signature.

In the past I would usually text Bud based on my emotions rather than praying about whether to go ahead with it. A few months earlier, I had sent him a text after praying for him most of the night, but he did not respond. I have since begun to understand timing. I was surprised to receive a text from him one snowy evening in March, but I figured his nieces must have shown him the book. I was glad to hear from him. He congratulated me for going ahead with publishing, and said he was very proud of me. We texted back and forth for a good while that evening. I had decided to give him a copy of the book, so we talked about getting together soon. After we said goodnight, I began to cry with heartfelt thankfulness for God's mercy, grace, and love. In spite of everything, Bud was sweet and thoughtful to me. He was not obliged to do that at all. I thanked God for knowing how to reconcile us, even if just for this purposeful moment. God can orchestrate a reconciliation between people better than any human being can plan it, period. Bud did not mention any of my old texts, but I did not hear from him again for weeks.

I had an embarrassing moment sometime later, when I accidentally FaceTimed him and did not know how to end the call. My phone was recording a video of me frantically trying to figure out how to turn the dang thing off! I texted to let him know the video was accidental. He later replied with a smile saying he was going to watch it anyway. Oh my goodness!

In March, a friend at work asked me about my proposed trip to Africa, which spurred me on to complete my application. I put a down payment on the trip, in faith, believing that I would have enough money to cover the cost. Within two days, I received an acceptance email. I felt like I was on my way to Mozambique! I sent prayer cards to family and friends. This was part of a 27-year-old dream! God was speaking to loving supporters, and finances began to pour in for my trip. I was amazed and in awe of God's goodness! Though I had many financial supporters, I ended up paying a lot out of pocket toward the trip.

First Trip to a Book Fair

On April 11, I arrived in L.A. for the International Book Fair. The night before the event, I went with a friend and her mom to Universal Studios. We were enjoying ourselves, but they wanted to go to the Harry Potter side of the park. As soon as we got there I sensed a shift in the atmosphere. My friend and her mom got a seat together for one of the rides and I sat alone as I went through the very dark ride. I was not afraid but I did pray. Many people do not realize that there is a dark realm but it is not as powerful as Lord God's realm of light, love, and peace. Later on, we had a delicious dinner at a seafood restaurant; I was very appreciative.

My friend came with me to my lodging in L.A near the book event. We were pleasantly surprised to find the place so clean, quiet, and safe. I made a mental note to stay here again if I came back to Los Angeles. The next day, we arrived at the book event just before it began, and located the tent that had my book on display. We took a picture of me with my book. While there, I met a fellow author, a pastor, who also had books on display. He encouraged me to keep my head up, saying that God had such great plans for me. As I walked around, I saw some veterans who had books on display. I talked with the men. One of them was a believer. He had been traveling to different places in the world to spread his faith. I bought his book and also bought a book for my Pappy. Before I left the tent, the man prayed for me since he heard that I was heading to Africa. His prayers confirmed to me how God was going to move in miracles in Mozambique. As I wandered around, I noticed a children's book display. The author gave me her card and showed me an amazing children's book group that authors could follow on Facebook. I was so grateful to check out the tips from the discussions. I still follow the tips online to help me move forward. My take-away was that I could pay for my own tent to display my books the next time I was at the L.A. Book Fair.

The next day, I went back to see my book in the show-case one more time. After spending another hour at the book event, I took an Uber ride to Santa Monica beach to get salsa at my favorite Mexican spot. I enjoyed sitting outside listening to the waves crash onto the shore. I heard a man singing songs on the boardwalk as I sat there, relaxing. Later, I went down to the beach. I passed a number of vendors as I walked along the sand. Suddenly, I saw a man walking along, carrying a humongous snake on his back! Eek! I had never seen a snake on the beach before. The man was charging five bucks to have a picture taken with him and the snake. No, thank you! I began chuckling as he approached different people, asking if they wanted to pose with him and his pet snake. As he walked away, I took a picture of him with the snake draped over his back. That was quite a sight. I walked on the beach for about an hour, and when the weather became overcast, I took an Uber back to the book event.

An Unexpected Distraction at Target

I stopped at Target to charge my phone. I found an outlet near the café, in an effort to stay safe. Two people were sitting near the outlet. I sat down, too, and plugged in my phone. Pretty soon an attractive man came over and sat down next to me. He smiled and plugged in his phone as well. His name was Teco. He was in L.A. as part of a travel club, attending an event with various speakers. I told him about the book event and my book. We stayed in the café almost two hours, talking easily to one another about life experiences. I realized it was getting late, so I asked him to walk over to the book event with me. The event was winding down, so we sat on a bench to talk some more. I enjoyed looking at him, noticing his handsome face and nature. We exchanged numbers and he walked me to my Uber. This meeting with Rico was a pleasant surprise. I smiled all the way back to the hotel, and all the way on the bus to the airport. Rico texted me that evening, saying that he hoped I had a safe flight back to PA. He was on his way back to Atlanta, the next morning. When I returned home, Rico and I were on the phone a lot, talking for hours. I really enjoyed my conversations with him. Again the following weekend, we spent a lot of time on the phone. Our conversations made us laugh, but I was also listening and picking up other subtle points about him. He mentioned how he tended to get lost in his work, and I kept that thought in the back of my mind. He continued to text me occasionally to see how I was doing.

One issue I wanted to address was the way our conversations were changing. He started calling me late at night, and those late-night conversations were getting to a point where lust was creeping in. I knew it and began to process this with God. I apologized to Rico for my own actions. The subject matter of those late-night talks had to shift. We continued our phone conversations right up to the time of my Mozambique trip.

An Impromptu Road Trip

Near the end of the month, I sent in the paperwork for my travel visa. By May 4th I had to resend the photos and my actual passport, since I had mistakenly sent only a paper copy to the government. Oops. Now the visa was going to take approximately three weeks to process. I felt nervous that it wouldn't arrive in time. I also began to pack for the trip, which I had already told Rico about. He was proud of me for going to Mozambique. He knew that the trip was going to be life changing. However, once again, our late-night talks were straying down an inappropriate path. God was showing me what I was willing to allow in my life. My heart needed transformation in this area and He gave me that correction.

The week before I left for Mozambique was both stressful and challenging. I was still awaiting my visa, which was supposed to arrive on the 23rd; but on the 23rd I found out it would not arrive until the morning of the 25th. That was cutting it a little too close, so I took the option of picking the visa up in Washington, DC, and took a half day off work to drive down and get it myself.

One important part of my impromptu trip down to D. C. was that I had the honor of meeting a man named Charlie when I stopped for lunch. I saw him sitting on the ground outside Chipotle when I came outside with my food. At first, I asked him if he needed any food. He said no, thank you, that he was all right. I went over and sat near him. He said he was a veteran. He told some details of his history, but he was upset that his family did not understand his situation. However, he said he was getting housing and assistance. I prayed with him. If the only reason for my trip was to meet Charlie and love and bless him, my trip to DC was worth it.

The contact said the visa would arrive at the office at 3:00 p.m., but thanks to Lord God, the visa was already there when I arrived at 1:30 pm. The woman at the passport office said the visas arrived early that day, which was unusual. I was so thankful as I drove back up to Pennsylvania. God knew I had to spend the rest of the day with Him, talking, singing, and worshipping.

After I arrived home, I hurried to take care of the remaining items on my list, such as getting my passport notarized and collecting clothing that I was going to give away in Mozambique. I was stressing later in the evening as I rushed to finish packing. I had lost my debit card earlier that week and I wanted to pick up a mosquito net from my mom's house. My mom texted to ask why I didn't pick it up earlier that week. She was not being very helpful. I was feeling completely stressed out and I began to cry. Later that evening, once I made sure everything was in the suitcases, I sat down to text Rico and then he called me. We spent most of the evening on the phone, since this was the last opportunity we would have to talk before the trip. I had really begun to care for Rico, but I could see we were not equally yoked in an emotional or spiritual way. God had been showing me red flags along the way. If anyone can learn from me, I would advise that if they get red flags from God, they would immediately listen to Him and do what He says. God knows how to protect us and He knows what is best for us. God's best for us is within His perfect will. We do have free will to stray but something will always be missing.

A Dream Come True

On May 25, I ventured out on the first day of the beginning of my life transition. This was the beginning of a

new love story with God. My friend, Betty, drove me to the
JFK airport that morning. I enjoyed talking with someone
who knew how exciting this journey was going to be for me!
I had a small suitcase and roll bag for this trip. At the Emir-
ates counter, the woman did not charge for the two bags.
What a miracle! When I boarded the plane, I was so thankful
that the jet was such a bougie, expensive, aircraft with lots
of high class seating and food arrangement in comparison
to other flights I've experienced. The seats were so comfortable. There were ten seats across and a second floor for the
business class, with shower suites. The flight to Dubai would
be twelve hours long. Fortunately, I sat next to a little boy
and his mother that trip. My first extended flight went well.
My excitement grew as I arrived at the Dubai airport, which
was luxurious. My next flight to Johannesburg, South Africa,
would not be leaving for several hours. The next leg of the
journey was eight hours. When we landed, I was in tears at
my first sight of Africa. I dreamt of this land since I was elev-
en years old. Africa was a place called home in my heart.

At the airport, I learned that my luggage had been
routed to Maputo, Mozambique, instead of Johannesburg, so
I was without extra clothing or accessories for the evening.
I rode in a van to the hotel where I was to meet with other
members of the team. The journey was very exciting! Most
of the team members arrived at the hotel soon after I did. I
spoke with my new friend, Ron, right away. He was able to
tell that Holy Spirit was dwelling within me. Sometimes, I
do not realize what people see in me. I was excited to greet
everyone. We went upstairs to get settled and then convened

for a late dinner, where we began to get acquainted and build rapport. The team members represented a vast difference in age: some were in their twenties and other ages ranged into the seventies. I spent the evening talking with a beautiful young woman, also from Pennsylvania. As we talked, we were making heart connections.

Some Funny Business

After breakfast the next morning we caught a bus that took us to the airport for the flight to Maputo, Mozambique. I unknowingly stood next to the door in the middle of the bus, holding on to a pole and my bag. Midway, the bus door inexplicably began to open and I felt myself falling backwards. Immediately, I began pulling myself back up into the bus. Whew! I had been so close to a bus stop-drop-and-roll, quite possibly to be left there! I was chuckling with some of my new friends who saw it happen! Once on the plane, I also had the unpleasant experience of the attendants spraying the entire plane. I had to hide my face in my shirt because the smell was so overwhelming.

The flight to Maputo took less than an hour. The process of going through customs went quickly and I was glad to recover my two pieces of luggage. On May 26, we met the IRIS[1] Global Ministry drivers outside the airport. Ron and I

---

1. Iris Global Ministries is a Christian interdenominational missionary organization that provides humanitarian aid in Africa, the Americas, Asia, Europe, and the Middle East. Members of Iris seek to spread the gospel while performing humanitarian activities. Headed by Heidi and Roland Baker

sat in the back of the bus with the luggage above our heads.
Fortunately, none of it fell on us! As I looked around the
city, parts of Maputo brought back memories of Haiti. I was
already falling in love with the green trees, the sky, and the
people as we drove the thirty minutes to the IRIS compound.
Once inside, I saw many houses and lots of children. We
deposited our bags in our room. Five women were to sleep in
one room. Fortunately, most of us slept on the bottom bunks
protected with a mosquito net. Once we got settled, we had
lunch in the kitchen. We all got huge portions of food, and
quickly learned that you have to tell the cooks the amount of
beans and rice you want. Some group members spoke Portuguese to the cook. Later, our newfound friend, Julio, gave us
a tour around the compound. Many children were in the area
having fun on the playground. That evening, we met with
Carl, the leader of the team, and began to share about the
day. All of our hearts continued to knit together in love as we
prayed together as a team. I volunteered to lead the prayer
time. We prayed together daily at 7:30 a.m. and 7:30 p.m. The
first night we slept well, overall. I enjoyed breakfast with the
children promptly at 6:30 a.m. the next morning. A loud bell
siren went off as if to shout "Wake up!" in the morning and
"Time for bed!" every night.

Following that first breakfast on base, we prayed at
the house of prayer. That morning, the children participated
in children's intercession. I began sobbing as we worshipped
the Lord God with the children. The younger kids all sat on
a mat in the middle of the room while the older children sat

on the benches around the perimeter of the room. After that amazing experience, I and two other women from the team went to the baby house to play with the little preschoolers. The babies sat in my lap and were having fun. At one point, a child took the toilet paper and began unrolling it. I lovingly urged him to pick up the toilet paper. He thought it was funny and was cracking up as I had him help me pick it up off the floor. But then he began jumping on the table. I knew not to reinforce his behavior with added attention, so I walked away from the table. Then one of his teachers came in and he got down. I had fun being on the floor and loving these precious children. After we left the baby house, we went to the home for children with disabilities. I was able to say hello and spend time with all eight children. One boy was having a seizure, so I prayed for him afterward. Before we left, we prayed for the staff at the home; they all received prayer. Lunch consisted of rice, fish, and veggies. During the afternoon, I enjoyed activities with the children. In the evening, we all decided which outreaches to sign up for that week.

Spending Time Out in the Streets with the People

On Tuesday, May 28, we got ready for street ministry, which involved leaving the compound and traveling to different locations in the city. We had a choice to sign up for street ministry throughout the week, or choose to stay at the compound with the children. I went on the IRIS van with the first group that signed up to go. Our first stop was to purchase bread from the bakery down the street, before we continued further down the road for a food called fried bean nuggets. Our first stop at the prison was to pray with the prisoners. We bravely had to cross the street as cars sped by in various directions. A guard stood at the front of the prison with a rifle. I smiled as we went past him into the welcome center. The police chief told us no one was in prison that day. I was in shock. This was so different in comparison to the unnecessarily large numbers of people in jail in the United States. Of course, there may be corruption in the city, but to have no one in prison that day was an interesting concept. One other funny thing to note was that I was wearing boots that were too big and clunky. For street ministry days, we wore long dresses and shirts. I can almost compare myself to looking like Popeye's Olive Oyl. It was quite the scene watching my boots lead me.

The Found Boys

Our next stop was to park in the middle of the city where there were boys who lived in poverty. They were referred to as 'the lost boys,' but I call them the 'found boys.' I was crying before we even got into the place. The thought that these boys chose to be homeless due to their home lives was grievous to my heart. At the entrance of the deserted parking lot, we had to go through a broken door. I literally fell inside the door due to my oversized boots. Once inside, I noticed piles of trash. Some boys, covered with dirt, emerged from the dilapidated structure. When I saw these precious boys, my eyes began to well up with tears again, and I inwardly cried out to God. The boys came over and sat down. The pastor spoke, then clapped his hands and all of the men present began to dance. Each of us did a fun dance in the middle of the circle. I was laughing and loving this dance time! Each of us had the chance to share the gospel. When it was my turn, the love of God was so compelling I got on the ground and looked in each of these boys' eyes. I told them God loves them and so do I. I took them by the hand as I told them this with such compassion and love. I said that Jesus loves them and comes to meet with them. As others were speaking to them, I had two pictures in my head. I asked if any of the boys had a bike. I had seen a picture of a black bike. The one boy answered that he had a broken bike. My friend Ryan said that the boy was sweet and kind and he had been hurt often. God wanted to fix the sadness just like his broken bike. The young man I was talking to was listening intently.

I went to another young man and asked him if a Ferris wheel meant anything to him. He said he was at a Ferris wheel recently. I told him that God loves to spend time with him even when he does fun things like going on a Ferris wheel. I hugged all of them and then we left. The boys received some of the bread that we had collected. The next stop was at another landfill in the city. I saw a mom and little girl and a few others in the area. Trash was burning nearby. We went down through some trash to stand with some of the people. The atmosphere was different here and I began to pray. As we sang, a man who was drunk was distracting the worship. All of a sudden, a woman came out from behind a huge tree with a steel rod, trying to hit another man in the tree. We prayed and left quickly. I was so sad because every person in that trash was truly a treasure. We got in the van and drove to a grocery store. Ron very kindly got me a French soda, which was refreshing. That evening, we met and prayed together as a team. A few of us went to pray over our leader who was not feeling well. I prayed for him during the night, and in the morning, he said he felt better.

On Wednesday morning, we ate breakfast with the children and then drove to the Hulene ministry, stopping along the way to get bread. Here there was a landfill so enormous, it looked like a mountain. As we moved toward the center of the landfill, tears filled my eyes as I saw family members of all ages looking for things in the landfill. When the people saw the IRIS van, they ran speedily toward us for bread. My tears flowed because they were all so precious and the need was great. We got out of the van, and some of us gave stickers to the children. We sang and danced with the people, as was tradition when the street ministry went to visit them. For ten minutes, everyone forgot their deep sorrows and pain. Ken told them about Jesus Christ's love for them.

Some of the women gave their lives to Jesus Christ. One woman took one of our leaders to dance with him in the landfill dump. She was so full of joy, I was clapping and singing, too. I went over to a man and woman who were watching and gave them both a huge hug. The expressions on their faces changed from sorrow to joy. We gave away more bread and then boarded the bus. As we drove away, I waved to people along the street. Many people were looking at the bus as we passed by. I waved at a hopeless-looking child and his father; their eyes began to beam as they waved back. I saw another man do the same thing, and then another. Tears streamed down my face as I told God, "There is so much need, Lord!" I was overcome by their brokenness. That was what Jesus had done for us—He became broken for our brokenness. He is our wholeness.

I was sobbing as we drove to our next stop, a church. Fortunately, we had enough bread to give to every person who asked for it! I saw children there and a man with Cerebral Palsy walking toward the church. I had such love for this man. I gave him a huge hug and he came into the church with the children. He sat in the back and the children came up closer to the front. Children clung to me. We began singing and worshipping, and I prayed for the man who came into the church with us. When we finished singing, we could either stay with the children or go around and evangelize people in the city. I went with two of my dear friends to speak to five women. They were sitting in the grass when we approached them. I gave each one of them an enormous hug. They were all desperate for love. We told them we loved them and assured them that they were not forgotten. Kat said they were world changers! Julio honored their culture and country. Later, the women hugged us again, and one of them asked us to pray continuously for them. Their request is written in this book for remembrance. I cannot wait to see what God does in them and within the community. We went back and sang again with almost forty children as we sat as we sat and listened to the gospel. I was praying for the little boy who sat next to me; I could tell he was deeply hungry for love from a mother and father. I prayed that the Lord would keep him and all of the children. Many children were gathered around me, and I spoke a blessing over each one of their heads before I left. I felt such deep, profound love for these children, and I walked to the bus in tears. We returned to IRIS, and then after lunch I prepared to teach Bible school that evening.

Words of Encouragement

As I sat there, one of the missionaries came by and sat down next to me. She asked if she could pray for me, and then gave me a word of encouragement for the evening. I then prayed for healing in her back and emotions. She sensed a shift after the prayer. I felt refreshed in my spirit and knew how to teach the lesson from beginning to end. Kat and Maria were coming to support me. Before the class began, I asked K to pray for a word of knowledge about any physical symptoms that we could minister to. Working through an interpreter, I talked about the kingdom of God and how Jesus asks that everyone come to Him. Then, I spoke about healing. I went through the steps for emotional trauma. K felt pain in his foot (as a word of knowledge) and soon one of the men came forward with that symptom. As I went through the steps, Holy Spirit worked and the interpreter, I sensed that the man was releasing emotional pain. The man knew that Jesus his surrender. We were not able to go deeper due to our limited amount of time, but the man felt a difference afterward. Praise God! After dinner, I was able to spend some time with Papa God, reflecting on the evening. When we returned to campus, we began prayer at 7:30 p.m., and then the team members began sharing about the miraculous healings God did during street ministry!

I fell asleep later than usual that night because I texted with Rico for a little while. The next morning after breakfast, we prepared for ministry at the hospital with a different street minister. Before we left, someone commented that the hospital was 'the best' in the country, but that most people went there only when they were very ill or near death. I had no idea what to expect. I began to pray as we walked through the hospital; it needed new doors and other essentials. There were eight people in each room. As we walked down the hall, we heard some people screaming in pain. I had been taught how to ask them if I could lay hands on them and pray. One man was very ill and coughed a lot. As I prayed, the peace of God came around him, and his eyes began to close. Another man was panting in great pain. As we continued to pray, his pain diminished. We prayed for approximately thirty people within a fifteen-minute time frame, and then it was time to leave. As we walked out, we saw families waiting outside, so we asked them if we could pray for them, too, before we went back to the bus. Once we were on our way, some team members were talking and laughing, but I began to cry with such overwhelming grief for the people who were ill and in great pain. My compassion for them was intense. I cried for a while, but eventually I was able to give it to Papa God.

An Adventure into the Great Unknown

I took some time to reflect and mentally process everything that had happened so far that week. I was also preparing for my weekend camping trip outreach. Four of us signed up to go on this trip; this was like stepping out into the unknown. In the morning, we went to children's church. I enjoyed dancing with the children. I was eager to see the children from the Hulene Ministry before leaving for the weekend. I did not get to spend much time with the children beyond a quick hug with one of the boys I had prayed for earlier that week. He remembered me, too.

Our team of four met the pastor at the prayer house and got in the back of the truck. Pastor Sergio stopped to pick up his wife and three children before heading to his church site.

When we arrived at the half-built church, we saw the square boundaries and the first layer of bricks in the middle of this land. Behind it was a church building without a roof. Pastor Sergio's wife helped us set up our tents on the land for the weekend. Three women were in one tent and our friend,

Rich, was in the other tent. Following the setup, Pastor Sergio walked around the perimeter with us as we prayed over the land. After the first time around, three of us went for a second lap while our friend Rich prayed in the middle of the field. I felt peace as I prayed, and I saw visions of God's angels on the land and the people who were destined to come to this safe haven. We all knew it was a house of praise and prayer. The stars in the sky were beautiful above the church building. Pastor Sergio prayed for provision, which reminded me of the story of how the three wise men began their long journey to see the Christ child, long before He was born. The provision for the building was on its way. Pastor Sergio was wise, realizing that each one of us was a part of the church and the building was only a gathering place. He has such a shepherd's heart and faith to move mountains. After the prayer time, we sat near the church, basking in the peace of God and His great goodness. Pastor Sergio, Ben, and one of the other leaders worked on readying the church for service that evening. They were trying to set up a generator, but it wasn't working, so the pastor used the light from his phone to set up the sheets around the walls where there was no brick to keep out bugs. Pastor Sergio said we were going to begin praying at 10 p.m. and continue for five or six hours. The weekend was certainly going to be a weekend of the unknown! Near 9 p.m., a few children and two women brought a table and set it with candles and food (noodles, fish, bread, and tea) on a red tablecloth. While they were setting up, I befriended two precious little girls. I tried my best to talk with them at the table. One of the girls simply stared at me. My heart was knit with their hearts. Pastor Sergio gave the four of us a place of honor at the table. After dinner, I went to get a quick nap so I could stay up all evening. My two companions in the tent were planning to get up for worship when they heard the people sing. I got up at 10 p.m. and went inside the church. There were about twenty people, adults and children, worshipping with some open space in the middle of the land. The love of God poured through this group of people in the middle of the dark evening. The air in the small open building became cooler as the night continued. God was in pursuit of our hearts. Raw worship and praise arose to the God of all salvation, deliverance, and healing. Everyone joined together in clapping, dancing, singing, worshipping, and speaking the Word of God throughout the evening.

At one point, very late in the evening, I began to understand something about what Jesus may have felt when he asked His disciples to stay awake with Him. This seemed like a similar situation. I was eager to stay awake and had the sense to do so. God was with us during this time to strengthen us. I found myself dozing, and then jolting awake at times, so I got up and walked around, dancing and clapping my hands in the wee hours of the night. It was glorious! At last, around 3:45 a.m., Pastor Sergio transitioned to the end of the evening. All of a sudden, we heard a rooster crow! I was so ready for bed at that moment, I was shocked that morning was upon us. I giggled and told K that I was praying that I would be able to sleep through the rooster's noises. We were trying not to laugh through the last prayer. After worship, we made our way to the tent, and all was quiet for a moment. Then suddenly, Children's Day music began playing, and a rooster crowed again! Kat and I laughed hysterically at the irony of the situation.

Fortunately, we were able to sleep, and when we awoke four hours later, we felt as though we'd gotten a full night's sleep. God is good. The only challenge in the morning was the latrine situation. I did not go to the bathroom in the dark, because the latrine is a hole in the ground that you had to squat over to do your business of any sort, for lack of better words. Although there was a brick wall around it, it was definitely not the most pleasant experience.

For breakfast, we walked up a short dirt road to Mama T's home. She was cooking eggs on the fire, as she did daily. The beautiful red tablecloth on the square table was for us four. We felt like honored royalty! She brought us potato fries, eggs, and bread with hot tea. The potato fries were delicious! The fresh eggs were from her own hens, and the bread was purchased from a local baker. Mama T has two small homes, a laundry line, and a latrine/shower hut. I said "Omegrado!" in Portuguese, which means, 'thank you' in English.

After breakfast, Pastor Sergio told us about the prayer needs of his team leaders; Mama T had stomach sickness and back pain, one fellow needed a miracle cure for his deafness, and two other men were searching for jobs. First, we prayed for one of the men who needed a job. I saw a prophetic picture of a man wearing a suit in a white building, which signified wealth. As Kristen began speaking, I had confirmation about the vision. She saw him as a man who was going to be wealthy in order to help the people in his community, the church, and others. Next, we prayed for the other man and saw him prophetically as a man of faith for his family. The next prayer was for Felicio, who had been deaf since birth. We prayed for him as Ron stuck his fingers in his ears for healing. I also had my hand on him to break any generational patterns and trauma. Carla was behind him and then kept moving further away from him, repeating his name several times and he would answer, "I can hear you." We began cheering and praising God! Felicio was able to hear in both ears for the first time!

Next we prayed for Mama T's stomach. We prayed for her to release emotional trauma (the sting of abandonment from four previous husbands), and then we prayed for her back pain to be released. After we prayed several times, her back pain left and the stomach pain had diminished tremendously. Her countenance seemed lighter and there was a glow in her face. One of us encouraged Pastor Sergio that God was healing his team for what He has ahead for each of them.

We then began our intended tour around the community. In Mozambique, the custom is to ask for permission to set foot on the land. Once the landowner agrees, they gather mats or chairs for everyone to sit down and talk. There were two teenage girls in the first home we visited. A team member had prophetic words for one of the girls, about how she was called to be a doctor who would help many people. I noticed the girl's sister, and we prayed for her also. She was called to be a teacher, and I knew God had great plans for her as well. I hope to always leave people with encouragement for their journey. Pastor led the conversation (all in Portuguese) as the woman at the next house welcomed us onto the land. The daughters of the house came over to sit down with us after a few minutes. One daughter handed her baby to my friend Kat to hold. After we walked away, Pastor told us that the woman with two daughters was a witch doctor. The first thing she asked while we visited was that we would not bind the powers of darkness. She understood that God had the power to defeat darkness. She also said that she was thinking about attending church. Witch doctors, who forsake the darkness to find refuge in the light of God's almighty arms, may experience rejection from their families and be forced to start over again. I believe her family will decide to come to the Lord soon. As we continued down the road from her house, we spoke with a man, a believer visiting from another country, who had been praying for someone to come along so he could receive a fresh indwelling of the Holy Spirit. He was astonished at how God answered his prayers! He was filled afresh as we prayed for Holy Spirit to overwhelm him. The man at the next house was a friend of Mama T's. He was housesitting to earn money.

One of Pastor Sergio's team members, Fernando (the man who was cured of deafness in both ears), began preaching salvation and baptism in the Holy Spirit. The house-sitter man rededicated his life to Christ and received a fresh indwelling of Holy Spirit.

As we arrived at the next house, an elderly woman hobbled out of her home; she was in grievous pain due to a knee injury. My compassion for her rose up and my heart wept. As we prayed for her, some of the church women went quietly to clean the inside of her home. While we were praying, God prompted me to kiss her knee. I knew this idea was from God, but it was a strange thing to do. I turned to my friend Kat and told her what I had heard and she said, 'That's amazing! Go do it!" I was about to do this when one of the women from the church was called to pray over the woman, and she was healed. I still went over, bowed down, and sealed her healing with a kiss to the knee. God is so good!

The last home was where we all gathered inside the small living room to meet Pastor Sergio's spiritual father, Peter. His appearance was sickly; he had been ill for several years and needed a blood transfusion. We gathered around the table, held hands, and prayed for him. We began to worship, which was a beautiful experience. I heard the Lord say something about pouring water on his head. My friend Kat anointed each of our heads with oil. This was the key for the pouring out of Holy Spirit. In the middle of the singing,

Peter began to weep as Pastor Sergio began to cheer and thank the Lord! Peter was healed! Pastor embraced Peter in such a beautiful hug between father and son; it looked like God hugging Jesus and us, as his sons and daughters. Tears streamed down my face in response to such a beautiful, poignant, and intimate moment of victory! We began to sing and praise God loudly for Who He is at all times!

Later, the group went back to the usual place we ate meals, at Mama T's, for what we thought was dinner. We had delicious food, bread, tea, and rice. As we began walking, they told us we would be back later for dinner after fellowship with Pastor Sergio's team. We laughed because we were so full.

Our team went back to the little church building to pray with Pastor Sergio's team. Fernando told us that since he was healed of deafness, he knew he had to walk with us wherever we went. He looked in on his mom and siblings but told them he had to stay with us and follow Jesus Christ as we went. That was such a beautiful reminder of the gospel! His team was greatly encouraged as we prayed for each person. Fernando received the baptism of the Holy Spirit, too. He almost fell backward as the power of God fell upon him. God moved on his team in an incredible way. We began praying for other team members and laying hands on them as well. The power of God works through any willing vessel. Our team had a private prayer time later, and our hearts were knit together as one, in Christ, through this trip.

The last evening of our time in Mozambique ended with a beautiful dinner at Mama T's home, sitting at the table with the red tablecloth. Dinner consisted of chicken, tomatoes, rice, beans, and a special pudding for dessert. We were treated like royalty by people who gave freely from what they had did not ask for anything in return. God was pouring out His love for us. I didn't know that my saying "yes" would reveal how much love the Lord has for His people and how He takes care of the little details. After dinner, we went back to the tents for a long, overnight rest. We planned to head back to the church in the morning. Every first Sunday of the month, all the local churches gathered together on the campus.

We finished packing up everything, and when the bus arrived, I sat by my friend Weeza, the little girl I met the first night. She wore my sunglasses, sat on my lap, and played with my phone. We recorded a video together and I held her tightly in my arms. God spoke to my heart while I held her; He told me He was always holding me like that, keeping me safe. I wept at this beautiful revelation of what it means to be a daughter of the Most High God. While I cried, the family of believers on the bus began to sing, and they continued singing all the way to church. I cried then even more because I loved each one of them and was beginning to feel the pain of leaving them. I was sad at the thought of leaving part of my heart behind.

Once we returned to base, I freshened up and went to find Weeza and the children. Kat and I sat with them and hugged our friends that we would soon be leaving behind. While at service, our group came up front and the children honored us with the gift of a capulana (a type of sarong worn in many parts of Africa). I cried once again at this kindness. God is so loving and kind. One of the girls was born with only part of a leg. We prayed for her and asked others to join in prayer. We could feel the stump growing past our fingers, and she said her leg didn't hurt anymore. I saw a vision of her running around on two complete legs, and knew that God was going to continue the healing process. I rested and wrote in my journal that afternoon. Papa Steve spoke to us about how the greatest miracle is loving children and watching them heal, some instantly, and some over a period of time. The miracle of Love is what spurs on every other miracle. God is my greatest Miracle and I love Him.

We spent Monday relaxing together in Maputo. After touring the city a little bit, we ended up at the market, which offered a variety of goods: paintings, jewelry, clothing, and hand-crafted woodwork. Many of us spent time bartering for good prices. I enjoyed watching my friends bargain for earrings and clothing. When we left the market, we had lunch at a mall near the affluent part of town. We talked a lot about what God was doing and had done during our time with Him and His people in Mozambique. Tuesday was the last opportunity for trips into the city. I spent time with the children on base but more time outside the base with various other people I met during street ministry.

To the People One More Time

One of my greatest joys in Mozambique was a chance to return to the street ministry to see the young men that we had encountered on the first day. I prayed that I would see all of them as we headed back to the landfill. When we arrived, my heart leapt to see my teenage boys! I saw the man in the red shirt once again, and a few new people. At least seven of them came to dance with us and hear the gospel! After we danced, we told them about our experiences that week. I said I was glad to be back and that I loved them. I asked them to close their eyes and ask God to show them a picture. The man in the red shirt saw a picture of himself taking care of sheep! He had the heart of a pastor. He was the only one who saw a picture. My prayer was that God would reveal Himself to all of them. After I gave them hugs, my friend Donna had a word of knowledge that someone there had foot pain. She said the pain was in her left foot and the man in the red shirt answered that he had hurt his foot earlier that day! We prayed for him and God healed his foot! He was amazed because his foot was no longer hurt and he began to dance and hug us! They enjoyed the delicious food we had brought for them. I love these "found boys" so much!

Our next stop was at the second landfill. This time, more people were sober and willing to hear the gospel. We did not stay long, but we were able to sing and tell them our names and that we loved them. The atmosphere shifted a bit, but the people just needed to be loved and recognized. They also received food for Children's Day, and then we went on our way to the last stop at the stairs at one of the outreaches with the men. Children's Day is an annual day to celebrate children. There is dancing, singing, and gift-giving to children. I missed going to this stop the week before because I was preparing to teach.

The final stop for ministry in the city was a stairwell outdoors where over twenty men came and sat down. One man asked me to sit near him. As we sang, one of my friends spoke of the gospel with passion and clarity. I felt as if I were hearing the gospel message for the first time. I was moved by what Jesus Christ did for every human being—His love is very far above our understanding! The men accepted the meals we had brought, and we left to get more souvenirs at the supermarket.

Following this adventure, we returned to base for one more prayer session together; this one was so powerful. Holy Spirit began moving very strongly on us all. I laughed hysterically with the Lord! We ended by praying for each other and then returned to pack. My heart was full. I spent the remainder of the time journaling, sleeping, and talking with other team members until we took the bus back to the airport. When we reached the airport in Johannesburg, I had my first salad in over a week, which was delightful! Ron prayed over my thyroid and felt the power of God released for deep healing within me! I will always receive prayers for health and wellbeing! God did heal my thyroid that day and I thank Him! He continues the healing process. I am so in love with Him!

I was one of the last team members to leave the airport. I waited, praying that I would get first class or an open seat next to me on the flight, which I was able to have on both flights. When I landed in New York, I was humbled as I looked back on my recent experience and I felt so thankful for God's great joy, peace, love, and safety throughout the trip.

God is Always Able

I felt such a change in perspective and a sense of the peace of God hovering over my life after I returned home. I continued to write about my life's journey while I recovered from jet lag. As I processed my thoughts and emotions, I began to realize that I was confident in God's ability to deliver and protect me. My desire is to do nothing by myself, but to continue my life through oneness with Jesus Christ. When I am in complete union with Jesus Christ, I don't strive in great effort to do anything. Every area of my life receives a touch in His healing light.

During the first week home, I began to ask God to reveal Rico's heart in any area I hadn't noticed yet. After our talk on Monday, Rico said he was going to call me the next day. I feel that people should do what they say they are going to do. He didn't call me on Tuesday. I texted him in the early afternoon on Wednesday, asking if he was doing okay. Immediately, my phone rang. I did not start the conversation by asking why he didn't call when he said he would. He said he was heading to work in a few hours. He talked about his frustration with work and that he wasn't able to get to New York. I sensed that he was tired but the minute I mentioned it, he became angry. He was upset that I didn't understand. I listened to him complain about how he couldn't get to New York and wish for greater finances. I said I was glad we were talking. Then I mentioned the fact that he hadn't called when he said he would and explained that had been the reason I'd texted—to see if he was okay. He was immediately upset by that and began yelling. I asked him to lower his voice and to stop speaking over me. He became even angrier then, and said he was not going to speak to me for two more days and that he would call me on Friday. I tried to explain that I didn't understand this, but he became angrier still, and hung up the phone! I was in shock. After processing this moment, I texted him to say that his behavior was unacceptable and that I was not willing to put up with it. He didn't reply. After five days, I texted him to see how he was doing. In the text, I let him know that I did care for him and was willing to respond, should he decide to reach out. He didn't respond and weeks went by. I spent one night crying about his lack of response and then I gave it to God. I prayed that God would show me Rico's heart and my own. Suddenly, I began to realize this man was a distraction before my trip to Africa because I had spent more time talking to him rather than digging deeper into the word of God as I had been doing before that. I felt peaceful about the end of the relationship. I blessed Rico and prayed that he would be well on his journey with God.

Complete Wholeness

Internal wholeness has been an arduous and complex process, and I have seen great strides in me, but I had yet to see the effects on my physical being. Often, I grew frustrated by the slow pace of progress; during these periods, I spoke about my exasperation with Papa God. I had a vision of losing all the excess weight in the spirit realm, but that was not yet evident in the natural. I have such empathy for people who are struggling to improve their health and haven't seen satisfying results. I have certainly felt judged by others in this area of my life that was a painfully deep wound.

Before I left for Mozambique, God gave me guidance for what I was to do regarding my eating habits. I was asking questions, and He was answering me. I knew that this guidance was for my next steps and God's answer for my calling. God confirmed His word a week later by speaking to me once again. The answer was the same. I was to change to a plant-based lifestyle of fasting and praying. I wept, knowing I had not been obedient to His instruction. I prayed for a change of heart to be able to trust Him in this situation. God is good and if this was His best plan for me, I needed to move forward in this next step to begin the journey.

I began to experience shifts in my heart that summer toward the Lord God and in my healing. God was healing deep father-wounds and deep trauma wounds, but my next journey was to go into the deeper wounds of soul trauma. My hope is to be able to support others who are processing through deep darkness and the pain resulting from traumatic life events.

In the fall, I began my counseling courses, and during this time, my trust in Holy Spirit strengthened. The focus was to continually change my heart attitude toward the Lord. I felt braver and bolder to walk around my neighborhood and love people well. I also met many people from Africa again that summer at Lehigh. My heart was still in a deep healing process, but the power of God continued to surge within me as I ran toward Him in deeper trust.

Seeing Love Again Face to Face

I had finally come to a place of healing to such an extent that I was able to see Bud in November. This was the first time we had seen each other after two years of mutual avoidance. God knew it was time to set the stage for an initial reconciliation and healing. I prayed before I left my house because we had not ended up meeting earlier in the year as he had said would happen. I also did not know what to expect or whether he was going to bring someone, but I had an inner knowledge that Bud and I would both receive honor and not shame.

    I went early to his sister's home and brought some gifts and a game to celebrate her new home. I was glad that I was involved in playing the game when Bud and his current partner came through the room. My stomach flipped over the moment I saw him, but I kept my focus on the game and the girls. Later, he came downstairs and walked over to give me a hug. Even after such a long time of being away from him, I could still instantly read him. I felt so pleased to see him in person. Later, I went up to the kitchen to get food. I saw him alongside his partner and some family members seated at the table. My stomach was in knots and I began to feel anxious as I put some food on my plate and headed back down-stairs. I prayed for strength and felt safe in finishing the game with the girls. Shortly after talking with the girls, I knew it was time to leave. I gave the girls a hug and went upstairs to say goodbye to his mom. I saw Bud looking in my direction. I spoke briefly with his dad and noticed Bud glancing over my way again. I started to leave but as I walked across the room, Bud quickly stood up and made his way toward me. I tried to pass by him; we had somewhat of an awkward dance until we faced each other near the stairwell. I glanced down at first, but the moment our eyes met, it felt like forever and a day. Our eyes were riveted by each other and expressed a thousand thoughts without a word being spoken. No one can escape deep love; it always remains. In that moment, I knew that Bud still loved me and that I still loved him. Finding someone who sees you at your darkest and still falls for you in a surprising manner is a rare occurrence. I was able to discern where he was at spiritually, but I could always tell with him. I felt as though we were the only ones in the room. I kept my gaze fixed on him and then began to talk about his recent dissertation. My eyes spoke what my mouth could not. I felt safe with Bud but my anxiety in this situation erupted as I continued to talk with him, telling him about events in my life. I managed to keep most of our discussion to small talk topics, which wasn't nearly as deep as our conversations usually got. Bud told me that working with trauma clients was difficult and challenging. I knew, deep down, that there was much more he was about to face, but not quite yet.

At some point, I saw his partner come near, but Bud did not flinch. God was protecting and honoring me, and Bud did the same. He did not have to do that but he chose to in that moment. I had been willing to honor Bud by meeting this man, even if doing so would cause my heart deep pain and grief. The love of Jesus Christ in me was ready to be extended. However, in this moment, Bud kept his eyes on me and did not move his eyes from my gaze one bit. His glance and stance toward me was one of protection and I felt it. I left the house with honor. I don't know how Bud felt, but I prayed for honor.

I fell more in love with God; His response to my prayer and His great protection of me in that most uncomfortable situation were comforting. I praised Him and felt His peace. I was surprised that the evening ended with some semblance of reconciliation with Bud, even if our hearts were still in need of deep healing. God held both of us on our journeys. I trust God's perfect will even as I step out daily to learn it.

Boldly Moving Forward into the New

I am currently moving forward in my journey. I am someone who loves God deeply; I am thankful for who He is and that I am His forever. I know that my path is taking a turn around a new bend that is unknown, yet exciting! I am making deep progress in using the Sword of the Spirit to cut down all ungodly associations and lies. Jesus Christ is my Savior, Deliverer, Healer, and the Lover of my entire being. I am so grateful for Who He is and that He loves and chooses me always.

I have one final piece that wraps up all of my life until this point. To those of you who have chosen to read this book, know that it was not by accident. I hope you receive healing and will move forward as a loving and peaceful world-changer! God commissioned me in a deep sense, and He has greatly changed my heart to align with His. I am ever grateful for His loving kindness and mercy, which is new daily.

In July, I began to experience the Holy Spirit in a deeper way, and I knew it was time to run in the Holy Spirit as a forerunner of Jesus Christ, Who is the Living One, Who saves heals, and delivers people today. In my spirit is simply, "Change the way you think, prepare the way of the Lord Jesus Christ! Leave everything and go back to your first love in Him!"

The Journey Synopsis—the Girl He loves

Before she was put into her mother's womb, Papa God looked at her with adoration and love pouring from His eyes. His eyes and voice spoke, "I love you, My beloved daughter. Remember who and whose you are, once inside the womb. Do not fear, beloved; you are Mine and I am yours. I will always be with you. Keep seeking me and you will find me again." Inside the womb, everything was new. Papa God never left her, but this environment was different. She felt darkness for the first time and a sense of separation from Papa God. During those early years, Papa God still made His name and character known, even in the darkness. Beloved spent many nights calling to Him, especially on the darkest of nights. Suddenly, the darkness and lies became more familiar than her Beloved Heavenly Father. The little girl was in the darkness and in such sorrow without being able to understand why her heart felt so sad. She thought Papa God had left and she felt heart-broken. Her earthly father was not like what she remembered of her Heavenly Father, who loves and treats her well. At times, Papa God elevated her as a princess in weddings. He spoke to her in songs when she sang, Jesus loves me. This little girl was still unable to connect fully. She was self-protecting and unable to receive the very thing that was supposed to heal her broken heart—the deep love of the Father in all the deep wells of her mind, heart, and soul. Throughout the years, this girl began to believe she deserved torment, confusion, and hurt. The ongoing theme in her life was that she was not worthy of love. Everyone in her life spoke words that hurt her heart deeply, like daggers plunged deep into her heart. She longed for her Heavenly Father. In a frail attempt to ease the pain, as the girl grew, she ran to boys, food, sex, masturbation, anger, work, achievement, friends, and fantasy to try to relieve the pain of her sorely grieving heart. None of the false idols gave her the comfort she needed in her life. At times, she saw glimpses of her loving Father. She had to undo all of the lies that she was acquainted with in the world. Papa God was constantly in pursuit of her. He was there during abuse, rejection, abandonment, grief, joy, sadness, pain, and deep heartbreak, and He was never going to leave her. Following years of His pursuit, this beloved girl made eye contact once again with the Lover of her soul, her beloved God. The look in His eyes softened her heart and reminded her of His love and care for her. She began to spend time with Him and receive His great love back into her heart. Papa God's relentless pursuit of her heart was amazing. She came back to life with His breath. Papa God's ability to love her mind, heart, soul, spirit, and being led her to glow in His glory and love. God's mercy and lovingkindness led this beautiful beloved daughter, changed her mind in repentance, and enabled her to adopt a better way: the Way, the Truth, and the Life. Over the years, God has spent time helping her believe that He is trustworthy and always good. He brings loving conviction and longs to have relationship with her. She will never receive any better love in her being than from the One whom her soul loves. The greatest Husband and the love of her life is the Lord God, her maker. Reveling in reconciliation and union with her truest Love, this beloved daughter began to dance with the Father as she placed her feet on His feet and moved with Him in unison. She is always thankful to Him and willing to learn more about how to love Him well. Papa God is worthy of all of her praise. As she discovered more about her true identity in Him, this girl glowed with His love by dancing, singing, and loving others. Her light, love, peace, and joy is Jesus Christ. She adores Him forever, in holy awe and fear, joyously spending every moment of the rest of her journey with Him. She will go with Papa God wherever He leads. This beloved daughter shines gloriously with His beauty, which illuminates her, inside and out.

Thank You, Lord, for loving me and pursuing a relationship with me, both now and forevermore. I will continue to seek You and enjoy finding You for the rest of my life. I adore you, Lord.

Silent No Longer

Invite Amanda to Speak at Your Event

Dr. Amanda Helman
International Speaker

Author, Mindset Coach, Speaker
Founder of Healthy Roots LLC
Coaching and Consulting Services

Dr. Amanda empowers people to be set free from limiting old ways of thinking to release their voice and vision to launch into their destiny. She is known for her passion, compassion, resilience, and words that both identify and release old beliefs. Dr. Amanda believes healthy connection and communication in personal and professional relationships are critical to healing families, generations, communities, cities, regions, and nations. She has a passion to set the captives free from painful events, acute trauma, and complex trauma so they can launch into their true identity.

Topics:
- Author Mindset Coaching
- The Power of Communication and Connection
- Complex Trauma
- Generational Trauma
- Trauma-Informed Practices
- Educational Leadership
- Mental Health and Wellness
- Personal Development for Leaders

Great For:
- Keynote
- Conferences/Summits
- Summits
- Coaching
- Consulting
- Church Service

Book to Speak
Call (610) 462-0167 or
Email: amanda@amandahelman.com

Made in the USA
Middletown, DE
28 November 2021

53636132R00169